Winter Forest

Winter Forest

A Devotional for Holda

Edited by
Heather Rohan Choppin

Hubbardston, Massachusetts

Asphodel Press
12 Simond Hill Road
Hubbardston, MA 01452

Winter Forest:
A Devotional for Holda
© 2022 Heather Rohan Choppin
ISBN 978-1-938197-29-1

Cover Art © 2022 Brandon E. Hardy

All rights reserved. Unless otherwise specified,
no part of this book may be reproduced in any form
or by any means without the permission of the author.

Distributed in cooperation with
Lulu Enterprises, Inc.
860 Aviation Parkway, Suite 300
Morrisville, NC 27560

I would like to dedicate this book to my disir, Odin, Freya, De Quita Bardwell and my father Lee Choppin.

Contents

Praising the Lady

   The Wandering Tale of the Winter Lady's Names 1
   Winter Hearth 11
   Riding With Holda 14
   Lina's Ordeal 18
   Mother of Witches..24
   Invocation to Holda 25
   Sweeping a Way..27
   Wild Hunt Invocation..30
   The Wisdom of Frau Holle 33
   Interview with Tchipakkan 2021..36
   Invocation to Perchta 40
   Berchta: Ancient Alpine Goddess 41
   Perchta, My Teacher 48
   Lady of Hounds 50

Holda's Rites

   An Altar for Holda..55
   Holda Housecleaning Rite 56
   Lessons From the Lady of the Look...58
   Cooking With Holda 71
   Twelve Days of Holda's Yule 76
   For the Hearth 79
   For Elderflower Wine 80
   For Good Cooking...81
   For Cleaning the Chimney..82
   For a Besom 83
   Blessing a New Basket..85
   For Spinning 86
   For Weaving 87
   For Soapmaking..87
   Holda's Elderberry Potion 89
   Another Elderberry Charm for Holda.......................................92
   Our Yule Holda Rite 93
   Holda's Sacred Places...96
   Holda Mantra and Yantra 101

Foreword

My first vision of Holda occurred while I had been practicing Golden Dawn ceremonial magic and working with the Egyptian pantheon for thirteen years, during a solitary Golden Dawn ritual. I did not know much of anything about Germanic and Norse mythology, and it would only be over the following month I would learn more about my vision.

I found myself in a snowy forest, but I was still dressed in my Egyptian garments and I wore the side lock of youth, worn by ancient Egyptian children. I believe I was being shown that my next spiritual level was about to occur.

I heard movement in the woods, and it was a sleigh pulled by two white stags, driven by an older woman. She stopped in front of me and told me to get in the sleigh. I refused because I had no idea what was going on. She was strong for an old woman, and she dragged me into her sleigh whether I wanted to or not. We rode through the woods until we came to a cave, which appeared to be a place of healing and magic. There were a few wooden tables, some cups, and lots of herbs hanging to dry. She ripped the side lock of youth off my head and I grew in a full head of long hair. Next, she ripped of my Egyptian garments and I stood before her naked. She looked me up and down as if examining me. She said "Upf!" and gave me a Germanic dress to wear.

We exited the cave and next to it was a spring. She shoved me into the spring, and I sank down and down towards the bottom. Instead of hitting bottom, I came out on the top of the spring in an alternate reality, in a different forest. In the middle was a huge tree that I would later learn was Yggdrasil.

I heard a clamor and got scared, so I shapeshifted into a squirrel and ran up Yggdrasil. I saw an eagle and ran back down the tree thinking he would eat me. When I hit the ground, I turned into a rabbit, and the eagle swooped down and picked me up. I shifted into a snake so I could slither out his talons. I then shifted into a horse and tried to gallop away.

Edited by Heather Rohan Choppin

I saw a group of dead ghosts, led by spirits I would later learn were Wotan and Holda, charging after me. As soon as they caught up with me, I awoke from the vision, finding myself back in meditation position and having no idea what just happened.

The next night Wotan appeared to me at 3:33 a.m standing on the side of my bed. I did not know the runes at the time, but he gave me two runes which were flaming with blue fire: Gebo and Algiz. Holda appeared to me again that week, but this time she was an incredibly old shaman woman. For many years I had no idea who she was. I thought she was a separate being from Holda, but I learned she is part of Holda. She, along with Wotan, taught me magic and shamanism. This would start my journey into the Germanic pantheons, and twelve years later I am oathed for life to both Wotan and Holda.

For this gift, for pulling me into that sleigh and bringing me into this world of Northern magic, I have put together this devotional as my offering to the Winter Lady.

HEATHER ROHAN CHOPPIN
MARCH 2021

Praising the Lady

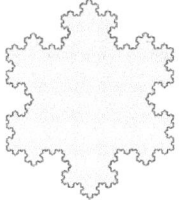

The Wandering Tale of the Winter Lady's Names
Raven Kaldera

For the past two hundred years, scholars have been peering into the ancestry of Holda's name, hoping to find clues to her own origin on that pathway. However, that has mostly led to speculation and a lot of blind alleyways, any of which could be the right road, but which remain darkened for lack of evidence. Holda's origins go well beyond literacy in the area of the Germanic tribes, and goddesses were less regarded—and thus less recorded—by outsiders.

The first problem is, of course, that she has many names—or aspects, or sisters, or cousins, depending on how one chooses to view these things. She is variously known as Holda, Hulda, Hulle, Holla, Holle, Perchta, Perahta, Pehta, Berchta, Berchte, Berta, Bertha, Gauden, Goden, Gode, Gaur, Gauerken, and Wohl, determined by which area of the Germanic region one looks at. While we think of Germany as a united country today, this is a purely modern situation. Before 1871, Germany was a collection of city-states, which grew out of a collection of tribal groups, each with their own dialect. Each was semi-isolated and had its own tutelary deities, including local ones who reflected their geography. Jakob Grimm tries to put Holda with the original Suebi tribe, later to give their name to Swabia, but this, too, is argued by scholars.

The first batch of names—Holda, Hulda, Hulle, Holla, Holle, and probably Wohl as well—may derive from the German word *huld*, meaning "gracious, friendly, sympathetic". This word comes from the Middle German *hulde* through Old Germanic *huldi*, which is in turn from the Proto-Germanic *hulþaz*, which comes in turn from the Proto-Indo-European *kel*, meaning "to incline or bend". *Huld* is also found in Danish and Swedish, where it also means "gracious". It is cognate with the Old English word *hyld* or *hield*, referring to the favor and protection of a superior to an inferior, Old English *hold* which meant "gracious and loyal", and Icelandic *hollur* "faithful, loyal". It might also have something to do with the similarly derived Danish/Swedish word *hylde*, which originally meant "to praise" but later became the word for "shelf", meaning something set in a high place. Here we see Holda as protector, especially of children and pregnant women.

On the other hand, it may be connected instead instead from the *huldra* or *hulder*, seductive but sometimes deadly forest-nymphs whose name comes from *hyld*, an old Norwegian word for "hidden" or "secret". This word descends from the Proto-Germanic *haljo*, meaning "covered, hidden" from whence we also get the name of the underworld goddess Hel or Hella.

Another possible etymology links Holda to *Hludana*, a goddess-name found in five Latin inscriptions in the Germanic area. Some scholars consider this goddess-name to be related to the Greek *Khludano*, meaning "high waves, rough water", perhaps a local water-deity. Yet another potential track is *Hloþyn*, an alternate name for Jord, the earth-goddess mother of Thor. (The etymology of that last name is still unknown.)

The second batch of names—Perchta, Perahta, Pehta, Berchta, Berchte, Berta, and Bertha—come from southern Germany in the Alpine regions. (Some people feel that Perchta is the same goddess as Holda; some that she is a sister or cousin. As I don't know for sure, I won't assume either way.) These names may come from the Old High German *berecht* or *bereht* ("bright"), which comes in turn from Proto-Germanic *brehtaz*. This supposedly echoes her White Lady form, the brightness of the sun on the white snow. However, an alternate etymology suggests that Perchta comes from the Old High German *pergan*, which means—like *haljo*—"hidden" or "covered".

The third batch of names—Gauden, Goden, Gode, Gaur, and Gauerken—come from the folklore of northern

Mecklenburg, where Holda was euhemerized in the tale of a woman who loved hunting so much that she declared she would rather hunt forever than go to heaven. She was thus doomed by God to eternally run the Wild Hunt, and her many daughters were changed into her hunting dogs, and also the dogs that pull her wagon or sled. In parts of Mecklenburg and Westphalia they tend to replace "w" with "g", and the name of the God-King Odin is Goden or Gauden. As "Frau Goden", she was a female version of Odin, leading the Wild Hunt. In northern Germany her hunt was full of the recently dead, but in southern Germany she led a band of the souls of dead (and, during the Christian era, unbaptized) children. One could see this as Holda being involved with both leaving and coming into the world. The other tree dedicated to her, besides the watery elder, is the juniper bush—supposedly for its use as an abortifacient; the keeper of the dead infants also aids women in shedding their unborn children.

The association with Odin led Jakob Grimm to decide that she was actually Frigga, Odin's wife, although there are no myths about equally-domestic Frigga leading a hunt. This is also the name by which she was associated with the harvest, at least briefly—the last sheaf was left in the field as "Fru Gode's portion", a bribe for better weather in the coming winter.

If we were to look at these potential etymologies not as "correct" and "incorrect" per se, but as an mysterious path of breadcrumbs laid by a goddess to make us think, we see an interesting grouping—gracious and praised; bright and yet hidden and covered; rough water and earth, dark night and bright white snow. Regardless of which of these is the original word, Holda still shows through as the Lady Under the Mountain, the Lady Down the Well.

There is also the matter of Holda's epithets, which while not proper names can still tell us a lot about her character. Holda passed from worship to folklore in the Christian era, and stayed around as an ugly old woman folk-figure in parades. We know that she became a sort of bogeywoman, the fate of many former deity-figures. In some parts of Germany she was known as both *Dunkel Grossmutter* and *Weisse Frau*—the Dark Grandmother and the White Lady. While may people will tend to think of "white" as meaning "good" (an association that is treacherous in many cases) in the far north, "white" was the deadly snow that fell every year, covering all life, synchronous with the long, dark nights. Holda, as the Goddess of the Winter Solstice, is both the deathly winter and the kindly figure one prays to in order to survive it. This is her weather goddess aspect—it's commonly known that the snow is Holda beating her feather pillows or featherbed, but it was also said that fog was the smoke from her fire and that thunder was heard when she reels in her flax.

Another epithet of hers is *Wasser-Holda* ("Water-Holda"), and here she is a goddess of wells and springs, the entrances to the Underworld. She is said to haunt lakes and fountains, and appears as a fair lady bathing in the water and disappearing. Her tree is the elder, said to be the guardian of the Underworld, which is often found by springs and bogs; the presence of elder trees means wetlands and high groundwater.

In Silesia, she is known by a variety of epithets involving spinning, including *Spillahulle*, *Spillaholle*, *Spiellahole*, and even *Spindelholle* ("Spindle Holle"). Further variants of this epithet include Spilladrulle ("spinning troll-woman"), Spillagritte ("spinning Gretel"), Spillmarthe ("spinning-Martha"), Spillalutsche, and Spellalutsche, the last two of which seem to mean "spinning-sucker". These all reflect Holda's face as the Spinning Goddess—specifically of flax culture. One of her myths involves a farmer stumbling into a cave in a mountain during a winter blizzard. There he finds a beautiful woman covered in gems and surrounded by treasure, but holding only a simple bunch of blue flowers. The farmer does her some service when asked, and she offers to give him a gift. He fears that the treasure is an illusion, and asks only for the bunch of blue flowers to give to his wife. The beautiful lady then turns into a crone and tells him that he was wise; the flowers are flax blossoms and to take them is to learn the secrets of flax culture. She later comes to his wife and passes that wisdom on to her. However, the price of the Spinning Goddess for this gift is constant diligence in the art; thus her "bogeywoman" forms that punish the lazy wives and children who don't get the spinning done in time.

In other areas, she is known in folklore as *Popelholle* ("Hooded Holle"), an old woman wearing ragged clothing with a hood. This led to *Zumpelholle* ("Rumpled Holle") which led in turn to the epithets *Zumpeldrulle* or *Zompeldroll* ("rumpled troll-woman"). Other names (in obscure German rural dialects for which I have been unable to find exact locations) include *Satzemsuse* (apparently "Leaping Susan" in some rural dialects) and *Mickatrulle* ("puny troll-woman"). In the *Satzemsuse* form, the old woman is accompanied by the *Satzemkater* ("leaping cat") and *Satzemziege* ("leaping goat"), and a crowd of dancing sprites referred to as *Rilpen*, all of which were once seen in local festival parades.

Perchta has many of the same epithets plus some new ones. She is called *Trempe* ("tramping one") and *Stempe* ("stomping one"), especially when portrayed in a parade, as Perchta and her costumed horde (sometimes simply referred to entirely as *Perchten*) are expected to make a racket. A similar epithet is *Rauweib* ("rough woman"). Some of her Perchten are *Schönperchten* ("beautiful Perchten") and some are the *Schiachperchten* ("ugly Perchten"), hideously deformed demon-creatures; this echoes her two forms as White Lady and Dark

Grandmother. She is *Percht mit der Eisen nas* ("Perchta of the iron nose") and *Percht mit der langen nas* ("Perchta with the long nose"), again describing her crone-form in the festival parades. She is *Berchta vom grossen fuss* ("Berchta of the big foot") or *Berchte vom Schwanenfuss* ("Berchte of the Swan Foot"), the idea being that she had one large, flat foot from constant use of the spinning-wheel treadle.

In the highly Catholic regions of the Alps, Perchta was associated with the Ember days, liturgical fast days four times a year, and some of her epithets were Frau Faste ("Lady Fast"), Quatemberca ("Ember Day woman"), and Fraufastenweiber ("Lady Fasting-Woman"). If people ate anything other than the traditional meal of fish and gruel during these days, Perchta would slit their bellies open and stuff them with straw. The Church apparently gave her the job of guarding the fast days due to her association with winter (the "lean times") and her existing status as the upholder of cultural taboos, such as spinning during the twelve days of Christmas. Like Holda, she would roam the countryside between Christmas and Epiphany, checking in on households to see if everyone had worked hard during the year, and that all the spinning had been finished by Christmas Eve. Lazy family members would, again, get their bellies slit open and stuffed with straw, or—if she was in a gentler mood—be beaten with the bunch of stinging nettles that she carries, another of her sacred plants. If she is pleased with the year's work, she would leave a nettle behind over the door to give protection from misfortune for the following year.

Finally, the epithet given to her by some Church fathers was *striga Holda*, or Holda the witch. Known as the Queen of Witches, she supposedly led gangs of broom-riding women to their nighttime rituals. The Queen of Witches was especially popular in the Harz Mountains, where Holda was said to stage her largest and most riotous yearly ritual on the top of the Brocken. The "kitchen witch" which appears hanging in people's kitchens as rustic art came over with the Germans to

Pennsylvania; she is yet another form of Holda the goddess of domestic arts, but also the witch who can use her cauldron and great spoon to create spells and potions.

Holda has been syncretized with multiple later Norse and Germanic goddesses, and consorted with multiple Gods. In Wagner's Rhinegold, he refers to Holda as another name for Freya, due to her part in the Wild Hunt, which is similar to Freya riding with the Valkyries. Frigga—another spinning goddess, this time in charge of wool-culture with her flock of heavenly cloud-sheep—has also been syncretized with Holda due to both that similarity and because she is a female deity occasionally associated with Odin. As the Lady of Elder-Tree and Underworld, hidden and covered, half-ugly and half-beautiful, Holda has also been seen as another form of Hella, the death goddess. The Church, who grouped anything non-Christian into one large puddle, associated her with Diana (due to her epithet "Lady of Animals"), Aradia/Herodias, and any goddess ever said to be worshiped by witches. In the area of the Tannhauser legends she is conflated with Venus; in at least one local area she shares with Venus the story of living under the Horsenburg Mountain with the faithful guardian Eckhart who keeps away intruders. In these stories, Venus's Eckhart is sent to run ahead of Holda's Wild Hunt, warning away intruders.

Just as she has many faces, she also has a number of male consorts. While later, more patriarchal paleo-paganism insisted that goddesses all be decently married, Holda is paired with so many different male figures that she still manages to retain the ancient privilege of the Great Lady who is not monogamous and chooses her own lovers. In the area of the Brocken, Holda was paired with a hunter-god named Holler, who is the German equivalent of the Norse Ullr. In northern Germany, she rides with Odin in the Wild Hunt. (Odin, after all, has many lovers, both divine and mortal.) As *Popelholle*, she is married to the *Popelmann* ("Hooded Man"), a Silesian bogeyman.

Alpine Perchta also had multiple consorts. As *Frau Faste*, she had a "husband" named *Quatembermann* ("Ember Day

Man"); as Berchte she is associated with *Berchtold*, a Herne-like figure who was also said to be the leader of the Wild Hunt. However, Perchta's most striking male-equivalent is none other than Krampus, the mountain-goat Christmas "demon" who was originally a local forest god. In fact, there is a great deal of overlap between *Perchten* and *Krampusen*, and both share the job of punishing naughty children. They are just part of a custom of wild figures that both embody and drive away evil spirits in folk festival parades. (For an excellent visual overview of these folk figures across Europe and Asia, I recommend Charles Frager's *Wilder Mann*.)

These names are all small pieces of her colorful nature, like brightly-colored patches we attempt to make into a quilt in order to see the whole picture. Generous and demanding, wild and proper, gift-giver and punisher, bright and dark, young and old, ugly and beautiful, high mountain and deep well, chilly forest and warm kitchen, childless and yet a protector of children ... Holda dances back and forth between opposites and manages, somehow, to bring them together. She is not a one-dimensional goddess, and she reminds us that we, too, have multitudes within us.

Winter Hearth

Suki Moyne

November.
I cooked my way through my sister's anger
At my choices. Her wrath split all the years
Of children's laughter, running in the old
Ball park together, taking turns winning at Scrabble.
Split it like cordwood to burn for her new life.
Don't weep, the old woman says, sitting on the stove
With all her long woolen skirts. *Bake. Take
Some of that fire back for your own nourishment.
You know, in the summer, how you hate to cook
And wish there were healthier meals in the freezer
Than in the store? Well, now is your chance.*
Two days I chop, mix, knead, watch the rising loaves,
Package like a thrifty housewife, until I am exhausted
And can no longer feel her wrath. The fire warms
My kitchen and my heart. I am not
Susie Homemaker, but it is better than weeping.

December.
He comes home from grad school, swollen with purpose
And eyes me warily. I try to interest him in hot soup,
But he is not fooled. The words fly, the moment I feared,
It is over before the bread is cooled. He goes to find
A motel room, says not to follow. I am like a wrung rag.
Don't weep, says the old woman, perched on the radiator
In her pointed red Mother Goose hat. *Clean. Go after dust
Like it was your life. Scrub until you bleed. Get him off you,
Out of you, away from you. Sweep until you can't stand it,
Until you can't stand up.* By the time the house is spotless
And I am reduced to mopping the pantry floor, his memory
Is strangely receded, as one months old and not just
A handful of days. For this is her gift.

January.
The snow falls like goose feathers, and I struggle my way
Through drift after drift to get to the job. Until the paper
On the desk about the downsizing. They are careful to make
The paper green, color of money, not pink, but it is the same.
Last slog home through that snowdrift, I look at clothes
In the store window, but do not dare reach for my wallet.
Once I would have bought them anyway, to hell with the
Electric bill, I will heal my pride with bright snippets.
Don't weep, says the old woman standing at my bedside,
Her silver hair misty against the shining brass. *Sew. So you
Are hurt, afraid, make yourself new armor, fetishes to
Ward off poverty and worthlessness. Fix the holes in
Old things, feel better about being a year older.*
The mending always piles up anyway. I stitch and mend,
My socks, my pride. It is not that I do not weep,
But you cannot wring your hands while working.
My frugality may be a conceit in this world of waste,
But it salves my heart like cool water. Not lazy. For once.

February.
He comes back to find some things he left, nothing
Important enough to have asked for before. I have
Thrown them all out already. I tell him to get his dirty
Boots off the mat and shut the door in his face,
Wondering at its arrogant bewilderment.
Why would I not value what he valued,
Put them aside to carefully return, in spite of
All his carelessness? The old woman does not speak,
Just cackles as the snow blows like feathers
From the roof. The goose is dead and cooked.

There are some who would say that her way is too hard,
There are some who would say that she denies the heart
Inside, stifles the tears that must fall.
They do not understand her ways.
She teaches me to pass sorrow through my hands
And into the work. The wash water is my tears,
The roar of the sewing machine my wail,
The thump of kneaded bread my blows of anger.
And then it is out, and there is beauty.
Truly, beauty is better than mere relief,
A wet pillow and a pile of used hankies,
And will keep you warmer in the winter cold,
And will scour you clean by Springtime.

Riding With Holda

Selena Fox[1]

You thought the person in the red outfit giving out treats to children on Christmas Eve was a jolly, overweight elf with a white beard and a team of reindeer leading the way. Nah. That's just what Santa's spin doctors want the world to believe.

Want to know who really decides who's naughty or nice? Try Holda, the Teutonic goddess of winter. She's the blonde wearing a shimmering gown and red or white goosedown cape who flies through the night sky on December 24th bringing gifts and spreading joy.

In Pagan religions, goddesses are an important part of our celebrations because they help tie us to ancient traditions and the seasons of the year. Holda is one of my favorites. Stories about her are found in old folktales of Germany, Switzerland, Austria, Holland, Denmark, Norway, and other parts of Europe. Her name means "kind" and "merciful".

I first discovered Holda many years ago while researching the Pagan origins of Santa Claus. In addition to learning that the Teutonic Gods Odin and Thor were part of Santa's mix, I found that in some parts of old Europe, it was Holda—not Santa—who brought gifts to children and determined who was "naughty or nice". I also encountered lore depicting her as dressed in red and going down chimneys to bring gifts to children. An old Germanic tradition included leaving an offering of food and milk for Holda on December 24th, known as Mother Night.

I decided to learn more about Holda, and connecting with her and her lore has been part of my Winter Solstice

---

[1] Used with permission, Selena Fox, Circle Sanctuary, http://circlesanctuary.org, http://facebook.com/selenafoxupdates

celebrations ever since. I invoke her in rituals, and keep a picture of her on my household altar. She is even among the Yuletide characters that appear in the public Winter Solstice pageant that I direct each year in Madison, Wisconsin.

As with many ancient goddesses, Holda is complex. Also called Hulde and Frau Holle, she goes by a variety of names and takes different forms, depending on locale and culture. In her form as a beneficent and noble White Lady, Holda is beautiful and stately, with long, flowing hair which shines with sunlight as she combs it. She wears a white gown covered with a magical white goose down cape. At Yuletide, she travels the world in a carriage and bestows good health, good fortune, and other gifts to humans that honor her. She not only is connected with Winter Solstice itself, but also with the holiday season that continues many of its customs, the twelve days of Christmas—from December 25th through January 6th.

In some tales, Holda is a weather goddess. Snow flies as Holda shakes her cape or the comforter on her bed. It is said that fog comes from her fires and rain from her washing day. In other accounts, Holda is a goddess of prosperity and generosity. Gold coins fall from her cape as she furls it. In one tale, after a villager worked all night to fashion a new wooden shaft to replace the one that had broken on her carriage, he found she had thanked him by turning the wood shavings from his work into gold. It was only then that he discovered the woman he had helped was actually the Goddess Holda.

In other early lore, Holda was a sky goddess riding on the wind. In some tales, Holda and Odin ride the sky together. Another of her forms is that of a night-riding witch leading a spirit host in a fierce ride, known as the Wild Hunt, through the sky and across the land.

During persecution times in Europe, some of those suspected of witchcraft were said to "ride with Holda". Her Pagan origins are evident in folk tales in which she is described as accompanied by a grand and furious procession of souls of the dead, mostly unchristened babies and children. It was said that as Holda and her entourage passed through the fields, they blessed the land with abundance and caused a double harvest in the growing season that followed.

In many places, Holda is closely associated with Perchta (Berchta), her tatters-clad shadow twin sister, also identified with the Wild Hunt and Yuletide. On Perchta's Day, January 6th, old Germans left offerings of cakes and milk on house roofs to bring good luck for the coming year. Holda and Perchta probably emerged as local variants of the same goddess-turned-folk character, since both sometimes appear in tales as hunched-backed crones and bogey figures, punishing or blessing adults as well as children for bad or good behaviors, at Yuletide and at other times of the year. As crone goddesses, they also preside over destiny and the cycle of birth, death, and rebirth.

Geese are sacred to Holda, and some say she is the mythological source of the storybook character Mother Goose. As the Lady of Beasts, Holda has many creatures associated with her, including hounds, wolves, pigs, horses, goats, bears, and birds of prey. In some tales, she lives in the woods and is the ancient half-tree-half-woman who gave birth to humankind. Apples and flax are among the plants sacred to her.

Holda also is associated with lakes, streams, and wells. In the Grimm's fairy tale "Mother Holle", she is visited by two half-sisters at her home at the bottom of a well, where she rewards the industrious one with gold but covers the lazy one with pitch. Holda as goddess of hearth and home presided over spinning and domestic arts. She also symbolized virtue, wisdom, and womanhood.

Today, across the United States, Europe, and other parts of the world, Holda is remembered, not only by folklorists, but by Pagans of many paths, who invoke her, give her offerings, and share her stories and traditions in Winter Solstice rituals and celebrations. As Holda takes her Yuletide ride this year, may she bring the world her blessings of peace, prosperity, and well-being.

Further Reading:

- ❖ Bates, James Allan, Doris Duncan, & Countess Von Staufer. *History of Santa*. Fullerton, California: Duncan Royale, 1987.
- ❖ Farrar, Janet & Stewart. *The Witches' Goddess*. Custer, Washington: Phoenix Publishing, 1987. p. 230, 260.
- ❖ Fox, Selena. "Frau Holda: Yuletide Goddess" in CIRCLE Magazine, Winter 2000, issue 78, p. 19.
- ❖ Guiley, Rosemary Ellen. "Holda" in *The Encyclopedia of Witches & Witchcraft*, second edition. New York: Checkmark Books, Facts on File. p. 160-161.
- ❖ Hilton, Edward. "Winter Goddess".
- ❖ http://des.users.netlink.co.uk/winter.htm, summary of "The Winter Goddess: Percht, Holda, and Related Figures" in *Folklore* Vol. 95: 11, 1984.
- ❖ Karas, Sheryl Ann. *The Solstice Evergreen*. Fairfield, Connecticut, 1998. p. 51-53.
- ❖ Leach, Maria & Jerome Fried, editors. *Standard Dictionary of Folklore, Mythology, and Legend*. New York: Funk & Wagnalls, 1972. p. 500.
- ❖ Monaghan, Patricia. *The New Book of Goddesses & Heroines*. St. Paul, Minnesota:Llewellyn Publications, 1997. p. 127, 252.

Lina's Ordeal
Raven Kaldera[2]

First, the planting.

The silver-haired mother sprinkles her seeds
From a gnarled fist; they are sown thick
That stalks may grow tall rather
Than bushy; thick together to hold up
Each other in wind and rain, not to be
Crushed by the occasional bird
Who mistakes the waving field of blue
For one of Her sacred ponds.
Grow, my children! Reach for the sky,
Says the silver-haired goddess who wakes the apple trees.

Second, the cutting.

The waving stalks crowned like the sky
Are to be cut down, each one at the hand
Of the snaggle-toothed mother with the scythe.
Each flax plant cries out; soft and delicate
As a woman's brow, her spirit is not sturdy
Like that of the waving golden grain. Lina weeps
And lies limply, cut off from the earth.
I am dying! she cries. *This is the end of me!*
Silly girl! Only another beginning,
Says the snaggle-toothed goddess who hangs the elderberries.

Third, the drying.

The stalks dry to brittle fragility, yet

---

[2] Originally published in *The Northern Shamanic Herbal*, Asphodel Press, 2010.

At their core is still a center of stubbornness,
An unwillingness to go where they are
Most needed. *See, I am delicate, I will break
At your touch!* Lina cries, in the hopes
That the silver-haired mother will leave her be.
*Oh, you are stronger than you say, my girl,
But I will have you yet. Just wait,*
Says the silver-haired goddess who rides in the wagon.

Fourth, the retting.

In her sacred pools the bundles lie,
Waiting in stagnant waters abuzz with flies
And kept company by tadpoles and the
Occasional passing frog. *I shall rot,*
Says Lina with some satisfaction, *and there
Will be an end to me. You'll see. It will serve you right,
For leaving me with such low sorts.* But a practiced
Gnarled finger tests the waters, an old nose
That was old when the Duergar first hollowed hills
Across the border of the world, sniffs the scum
And just in time, lifts Lina from her bed of slime.
I will cleanse you in clear lake waters,
Says the gnarled-handed goddess whose washing-day is the
    summer rain.

Fifth, the breaking.

The wooden brake lies in the hut's
Darkest corner; those gnarled hands
Life it out, dust off the elderberry dreams
And prepare the victim. Crack! and the shell breaks.
Crack! Crack! and Lina cries, *Enough!
My hard stem is broken, old woman,
Are you not satisfied?* But the grinning hag

Knows better. *Your core is still untouched,*
And thus you seek to hide it from me. I'll not have it!
And I'll break you still, my girl. Crack! and Lina
Yields to the hag who steals bad children, fills their
Dead bellies with straw and dirt from the cottage floor.
I will break you and remake you,
Says the tangled-haired goddess who leads the Wild Hunt.

Sixth, the scutching.

Lina is bent backwards in her torment
And the wooden blade scrapes her nerves—
I cannot bear it! she cries. *You can, my chick,*
And what is more, you will, for there is
No going back now. The ghosts of children
Dead aborning flit about that white-clad form,
As she peels away the last of Lina's defenses,
Hanging in tattered scraps from what were
Once stems. *You don't need this any more,*
Says the grey-eyed goddess whose hearth's smoke is the fog.

Seventh, the heckling.

Dragged through a bed of nails,
Lina does not understand why she does not
End, and have it be over. But no, the torment
Goes on, with no mercy in sight. Those hands
Are strong enough to drag her through the hackle
And gentle enough to rock the cradles of babes
Whose exhausted mothers have fallen asleep
At the fire, their fingers bloodied by too-industrious
Spinning. She loves them, the ones who work too hard,
Who push themselves, who are never content
With less than a spotless house, a perfect job,
Who let no discomfort stand in their way. They are

Her children. *You should learn from them, my girl,*
Says the gentle-handed goddess who midwifes dead babes.

Eighth, the combing.

They say that once a man stumbled into a cave
Under a hill, to be met by a jeweled queen
And her maidens who offered him riches.
They say that he asked only for the flowers
She held in her hand - perhaps he was awed,
And humbled, or perhaps he saw the old woman
Beneath, attended by ghostly babes, and thought better
Of any jewels. The flower was Lina, and his wife
Was the first to be taught of the journey, flower to gown.
She sings the tale to herself as she combs Lina,
Laying every hair straight and fine,
And who knows what version she sings?
Do you not like your new form?
Says the white-robed goddess who brings the first flurries.

Ninth, the dressing.

Cradled in the lap of winter, Lina knows comfort
For the first time, and true surrender
As the layers fall, back and forth, back and forth,
And rolled up around the distaff. *But I don't wish
To be bound,* she cries still, rebelling. *Hush, girl,
It will be over soon enough.* A blood-red ribbon
Binds her, for the mother's blood on the spinning.
Like the girl who fell down a well into another country,
Gave everything away, and gained the golden tongue.
Like her sister, who was selfish, and burped toads
Forever. *Which will you be, my chick?*
Says the snowy-haired goddess who guards the deep well.

Tenth, the spinning.

Here is where the magic is made.
The whirl of the whorl, the whirl of the wheel,
The spiral spinning that stretches time
And space. Outside, snow is fluttering
From the feather pillows she shook out this morning
But inside, all comes down to the humming thread.
Lina is silenced by the beauty of it,
Of time, of space, of the web of the Norns
Of which she is now a small part. *I understand, old mother,*
She whispers in the wheel's hum, and truly
It has all been worth it. *See, I have won you, my girl,*
Says the twinkle-eyed goddess who rides on the broom.

Eleventh, the weaving.

From Urd's game to Verdandi's. The threads
Cross back and forth, warp and weft,
Made beautiful, encompassing, a form
Like none ever seen before. The weights
On the loom are the skulls of babies
Too soon spat from their mother's womb.
The old mother works all winter, but not
Every day. There are houses to visit, women
To reward or punish, children to gift or curse,
Larders to inventory, grains of corn to count.
I am beautiful, Mother, Lina says. *I never knew*
I could be this beautiful, even in the days
Of the blue sky. I knew nothing then.
Only death and torment stood between,
Says the blue-cloaked goddess whose lace is the frost.

Twelfth, the wearing.

Stitched together with her own self,
Lina is open and ready, pliant to do the will
Of the broom-bearing mother. Baptized in madder,
Rose as the sunrise she waits. Will I lie
On the shoulders of a maiden, a man, a child?
It matters not—I can dream, but for the first time
I am ready for anything, and glad of it. Only death
And torment could give me this readiness.
I am open to the future, to wrap and caress
Any who will have me, with love.
It's for this you were born, child of the sky,
It's for this that you died, child of the earth,
It's for this that you suffered, child of the summer,
Says the winter-voiced goddess who waits for the spring.

(*Author's Note: Lina is the Saxon/Germanic name for the flax plant; Lina and Leac (Leek) were symbols of the archetypal female and male, much as we use Venus and Mars symbols today. Lina was the female equivalent of John Barleycorn who was sacrificed and tortured that we might live and was sacred to Holda. While John Barleycorn is still remembered today to some extent because we still eat grain, Lina is all but forgotten in this age of synthetics, as are the ancient steps for taming her.*)

Mother of Witches

Shannon Graves

Frau Holle, I would ride with witches
Out of my pale bounded life
And into the heart of your mountain.
I would straddle a broom behind
Your flying cart, sweep the sky
Like you tell me to sweep my house
Surrounded by the howling souls
Of dead children like scudding lint
Against the full Yule Moon.

Frau Holle, I would fly off the handle
And lose everything, to gain a fuller world
And your favour in the bargain.

I would mutter over my stirring pot
Instead of tinned soup and packaged noodles,
Or worse, bad chips. Teach me the potions
That will give me bravery, and more important
Motivation when the world is grey and dusty,
The will to get up and sweep again.

Frau Holle, I would do a hundred days of spinning
To pay for the spring cleaning
Of this one wounded witch's heart.

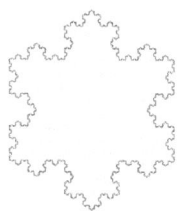

Invocation to Holda

From the Pagan Book of Hours[3]

Calendar of the Sun
17 Blutmonath
Holda's Blot

Colors: Brown and white
Element: Earth
Altar: On cloth of white and brown lay a spindle full of spun wool, a basket of white goose-feathers, two white candles, a needle and thread, a horn of mead, and a dish of honey-cakes. Lean a broom against the altar.
Offerings: Cakes buried under the earth. Organize and clean the house.
Daily Meal: Hearty stew with root vegetables. Wholegrain bread.

> Frau Holle, good Lady
> Of the Land Under The Earth,
> Who we reach through
> The well into the deep places,
> You who reward each
> As to the temper of the work
> They accomplish each day,
> You who have eternal patience
> And yet no patience at all
> With lazy fools who will not
> Lift their hands in another's need.
> Lady of the hearth, the loom,
> The spindle and the wheel,

---

[3] *Pagan Book of Hours*, Asphodel Press, 2006. https://www.paganbookofhours.org/

The needle and the cooking pot,
These things that so many
Take simply for granted,
They are your kingdom
And your warm domain,
And if they should be removed,
We would sorely miss them,
Much more than we could guess.

(*All approach the altar, seize handfuls of the goose feathers, and fling them into the air so that they fall like snow. Each then takes a turn with the broom, sweeping them up. The mead is shared and then poured as a libation.*)

Sweeping a Way
Brandon Hardy

When I started more seriously committing to a spiritual path, one of the things I offered up was my name. It was Holda who appeared to give me a new one: Brandon. While there are a number of reasons this name was chosen, and a number of possible translations for it, the earthy Anglo-Saxon version was the first she pointed to. There are a few places called Brandon, which is a mash-up of the Old English words "brom" (broom) and "dun" (hill). So one way to read my name is simply "a hill of brooms", or as my grandmother jokingly put it, "a parking lot for witches". While it more likely refers to the broom plant itself (*Cytisus scoparius* if you want to be fancy about it), I can't quite bring myself to dismiss her definition entirely.

The symbol of the household broom is a pretty universal witchy trait. It's not only omnipresent in pop-culture depictions of witches, but also still used today in modern magical practices. It's an item I strongly associate with Holda and her lessons of practical household magic, as it's both a mystical tool and literally something to clean the floor with. When she gave me this name, it didn't only spur a new interest in learning about how witches used brooms, it also came with a suggestion to start learning how to be the broom itself. Yeah, that sounds a bit silly, but I was enthusiastic and ready to find some kind of pretentiously deep, semi-metaphorical meaning in it. Instead I learned that this was already a concept long before it came to me.

Folk traditions are—thankfully—stubborn things, and when Christianity was at its height of snuffing out all the traces of Pagan practice that it could, some parts were able to fly under the radar through local traditions. One rewarding place to look for them is across Europe during the Yule and Christmas seasons, particularly in parades. Sure there's often a Saint Nicholas, but there are many much older beings celebrated alongside him as well. This is where you'll find Krampus, who somewhat recently became a fad hit here on the other side of the Atlantic, and even Perchta. If you look to the start of some of these parades, you'll find people dressed in massive bundles of straw, looking like an ancient ancestor of Cousin Itt. These are the brooms, albeit with somewhat proportionally stubby handles. Like a witch sweeping the physical and energetic muck out of their home's front door, these human brooms go ahead of the main players in the parade, brushing away the dust of the old year to make room for rebirth in the next.

It needs to be emphasized that they're being literal brooms—they're not clearing the way with a tool, they are the tool itself. It is by direct result of their bodies' actions that they are doing the cleaning. When I started to look at it this way, I found that the story of Holda preserved by the old Brothers Grimm echoed this sentiment. The girl at the forefront of the story was on her own path, but was only successful in her journey because she was helping to support the ways of others in need. When her step-sister tried to walk that path, a defining factor of her failure was being unwilling to do the same service. Her path crossed a multitude of other paths, and could only be done correctly if those were cleared as well. Then through her actions, their obstacles were swept away and everyone could continue forward again. Just as a broom could serve both magical and physical purposes, clearly anthropomorphized brooms could as well.

So here's some advice from a rather scruffy human broom. The next time you find yourself presented with a chance to help others on their path, take a moment to wonder if this is a gift (or a test) from Holda. It could directly affect their workload or help them avoid burnout. It could be something as esoteric as a magical working for someone in crisis or providing spiritual counsel, or as immanent as helping someone overwhelmed by their chores or giving a tired friend a shoulder rub. This could even be just giving money to someone in need—the folklore lessons of "mysterious old beggars" are not as lost to the past as we might think. Anything done with intent that helps someone better walk their path can be an act of magic, and if your path is headed Holda's way, you may find your own becoming swept clear as well.

Wild Hunt Invocation

Heather Rohan Choppin

Houses spotless.
Distaff lay down.
Shuttles in baskets.
Hearth fire burns.
Bread yeast rises.
Mead horn poured
For the dead and divine.
Tonight, they ride.

Old-time marriage
Wotan to Holda
God of winds
and Lady of Snow.
She fluffs the pillows
While her husband,
Shrieks in the wind.
Tonight, they ride.

In the sky
Plastered with stars
Wotan in blue
Astride the Eight-Legged
Among the clouds
Dead does he raise.
Howling wind.
Tonight, they ride.

Frau Holda,
Queen of Brocken,
Mountain and forest.
Across the earth
You punish the lazy

Reward those who toiled.
Fluff the pillows,
Making it snow.
Tonight, they ride.

Mother Holda,
Queen of the dead.
You surrounded
by Dead Children
You raise.
Mother you become
To the innocent.
Bless the little dead.
Tonight, they ride.

Frau Holda,
Will judge
If you have been
Naughty or nice.
Wotan will give
Great gifts of
Fright!
Tonight, they Ride!

Come one!
Come all!
Set labor aside!
Tonight,
Night of the dead!
They Ride!
They Ride!
Hail Wotan and Holda!

The Wisdom of Frau Holle

Crowspirit

"Anna, come here, *bitte*."

"Yes, Grandmother?"

"I need you to run an errand for me. Miss Tanya has a fever and is not feeling well." I looked over at the lady who has been our neighbor my whole life. Her ebony skin looked ashen and she was sweating profusely. "Take the offering bowl with some mead and the loaf of bread you baked this morning to the Elder grove and ask Frau Holle for some fresh elderberries."

My grandmother learned healing from her grandmother, and she was now teaching me healing and the old ways. Many of the low-income and uninsured townsfolk came to my grandmother for healing because the only doctor in our town charged more than they could afford. My mother had learned the old ways from her as well, but healing was not her strong suit. She and my father now ran the local kindred.

I gathered up the supplies and the offering bowl, and I quickly left for the grove. When I got there, I placed the bowl on the ground, poured the mead into the bowl, and broke the bread to release the energy, or *meginn* in the bread we had made that morning.

"Frau Holle, I know that Miss Tanya isn't one of yours, but she is a good woman and is in need of your elderberries for healing. Would you allow me to harvest some berries for her? I know some in the group would find her unworthy because of her skin color, but she has always been nice to me."

Just then the ground below my feet opened, water came up, and I fell through to another place. As I surfaced, I noticed an older woman struggling to carry an armload of wood to a nearby firepit. I couldn't allow her to injure herself trying to get the wood to the pit, so I ran over and offered to help. She accepted, and started a fire.

I noticed two chairs near the fire. "Are you expecting someone?"

The lady replied, "Only you, child; we have much to discuss."

"My name is Anna—where am I?"

"You are in my realm, and I know who you are. I have accepted your offerings. The bread was delicious and the *meginn* was energizing. You must have worked hard to bake it."

"Grandmother says we must always do everything to the best of our abilities, as we never know what will be needed and when, and for some reason I felt like I needed to put extra love into this loaf. Now I know why. It was for you, so we could help Miss Tanya. Will you allow me to harvest the berries? Miss Tanya may not be one of yours, but she is a wonderful woman."

"I know your grandmother well and she is a wise woman. You must listen to her and learn all you can from her, for there are not many as skilled at healing as she is. Have a seat, my child. I brought you here to tell you a story."

"I need to get back! Time is crucial to the healing."

"Time works differently here. What feels like an hour here is only minutes there. I will give you the berries, but I need you to understand something first, so sit down and listen to my story."

A long time ago, a soul came to my mill. This soul was radiant, but also disheartened by what they had endured in their lifetime. You see, that soul had endured many hardships, including being sold as a slave by a father who should have protected her, as payment of a debt to a village leader. She was used violently by many men, made to do hard labor, and demeaned by the villagers who used to be her friends. When her body could no longer take the abuse and the hard labor, she was cast out.

She died of starvation and hypothermia. She vowed to use her remaining lifetimes to fight injustice in all forms. In her next lifetime, she became a Volva, a seer, and she was able to bring about the downfall of an evil king. The next lifetime, she chose to be male and become a priest who was able to spread love, and foutght corruption and misogyny by the clergy.

The next life was spent as a mercenary for hire, but only to those who were worthy. In that life, he united four tribes under a single worthy leader. In another lifetime, she was a spy for the Allies in World War II. She hid many Jews in a secret tunnel on her property, and was able to pass along vital information used to defeat the Nazi regime, saving thousands of lives. In another lifetime she was able to end the terrorist cell which was about to blow up a factory. In this lifetime, she chose to incarnate as an African American woman to help fight for equal rights. She marched at Selma, she sat at lunch counters, she rode in the front of the bus. She was ostracized, spat on, and beaten a time or two, but she made a difference.

This soul has been many races, male and female, large and small, rich and poor, but always fighting for what is right, and always returning to the mill after each lifetime, waiting for another chance to make a difference. It pains me to think that narrow-minded people think I would not accept this brave and beautiful soul because of the color of skin she chose to wear in this incarnation. She has always been mine, daughter. Go and tell this to any of the kindred who would say otherwise, narrow-minded fools that they are. Listen to your parents and your grandmother; they know what is right.

She handed me a box of berries and then pointed me to the water. I looked back to find no chairs, no fire, and no Holle. "Thank you," I whispered as I jumped into the water and re-emerged in the grove. I ran back to the house, eager to let Grandmother know how special our patient really was.

Interview with Tchipakkan 2021

(Tchipakkan is a Neo-Pagan kitchen witch and organizer. She shared her experience with Holda at a conference and Raven Kaldera interviewed her later about it and transcribed the interview here.)

RK: So tell us about your Holda experience.

Tchipakkan: Well, I foolishly got to know Her better than maybe I needed to. This is an occasion of telling an embarrassing story on yourself, because it can be a warning. I am a historical reenactor, and I wanted to learn how to do everything that people used to do in the past. I got to the point where I wanted to learn how to spin flax, and I was also fairly well versed in folklore and faery tales and such. I went to a Pagan conference and attended a workshop where the presenters said, "For this class, we're all going to dedicate ourselves to some God or Goddess." I don't think that I got that intent out of the description, but since I was in the middle of it, I thought, "Well, I guess I could work with Mother Holle and she could teach me how to spin."

That part is true—I probably did learn to spin better because She was giving me a hand. However, one can't always expect what's going to happen next, because the Gods do what they do. We can learn about them, but we can't always predict the way it's going to work out with them. After I said, "Mother Holle, I would like to work with you," She started showing up. Mostly, the way She showed up is that I'd say, "OK, I'm tired. I'm going to bed." Then I could hear this voice in the back of my head, saying, "There are dishes in the sink."

I'd say, "I can do them in the morning."

And She would tell me, "No, you don't go to bed while there are dishes in the sink. And the table needs to be cleared, and the floor needs to be swept. Are you listening to me, or not?"

I would say, "Yes, I'm listening to you, but I'll do it tomorrow," but I could feel Her displeasure. And my goodness, She is emphatic! I have a feeling that would be true for any God that you were working with. If you were working with Kwan Yin, She may be compassionate, but She might also tell you, "You are going to go learn this new healing technique, right now!" Luckily, I learned my little lesson and I haven't gone calling up more Gods without thinking.

Mother Holle is everything you would expect an old-fashioned grandmotherly person to be. The traditional Gods and Goddesses were not always likable when the people who interacted with them experienced them, and She was not necessarily nice. But then She wasn't always nice in the stories, either. What I know about the stories might also affect how I experience Her—we can't know how much is our own filters. But I do know that with me, She was pretty stern.

I think that She finally gave up on me, because I am now able to go to bed when I feel like it, without the nagging in my head It wasn't so much that I got dumped by Her, it was more that we grew apart and we had a separation. I think that She would come back if I started diligently keeping house again—of course, She might have a few choice words or mental notes for me. "You know, you should have been doing this all along." And yeah, I would love to, but ... She gives you the skills, and She gives you the desire, but She's certainly not going to do it for you. This is opposed to the house-wights, who when you put in a good effort, sometimes do the work for you.

RK: Part of my work with Holda is that She is my house spirit. She told me that I don't get to have house spirits—She is my house spirit. But She doesn't do the work—She just reminds me that it has to get done.

Tchipakkan: Our house spirit has done repairs, and cleaned, and carried water. And we play cards with it—it likes that. Sometimes it even wins. Of course, you have to deal it in.

I think that when we are dealing with a large spirit—for example, our relationship with Thor, where we pour out alcohol for him—when you acknowledge them and you treat them well, then they are more likely to talk to you. It's easier to hear them when you form a relationship.

I think that's pretty much the end of my story. It's a good cautionary tale—don't walk into a workshop and randomly pick some deity. It's like that wonderful story told about the Gardnerians who tried to call down Athena, except that they were skyclad, and She came down and asked angrily, "Why am I naked?" You have to do the work to find out all about them before you start bothering them. Mother Holle was all about people who would bust their butt to help make the home a better place.

RK: Yes, She is a Goddess of labor in many ways, and She appreciates a strong work ethic.

Tchipakkan: I think She's a Goddess of creating comfort. It's not like She was doing anything mean; She just won't put up with laziness. I mean, frankly, I'm lucky that I didn't end up with a rain of pitch or snakes and toads coming out of my mouth! Because that's what's in the faery tale.

RK: Well, the snakes and toads were more about Her being angry with the young woman who was given an opportunity to help out people in need, and refused. That's a little different—it's a grade worse than just being lazy about housework.

Tchipakkan: Yes, the girl heard about the good luck of the other girl who went there and worked, and she said, "I want the gold." And when you work, you get the reward. She wanted the reward without the work, and no, that's not gonna happen. The thing is, you don't necessarily need a goddess for this—the reward for cleaning is that you get a clean kitchen, a clean house. You get the good food!

When I was spinning the flax, I knew that traditionally spinners were supposed to finish up the year's supply of flax before the Distaff Days in midwinter, and then you could take your break, but you had to get it finished first! And I remember that I didn't finish because I was busy doing other things. I think that was when I was officially let go and got my walking orders.

So that's my experience with Holda! I still respect Her, and I value what I learned. And now I can pass this lesson along.

Invocation to Perchta

Heather Rohan Choppin

I am known as the Belly Slitter.
Old Hag, who eats bad children
And scrapes out their eyes with glass.
These are lies the conquerors told you.

My name means "Bright One"
Birch trees are mine.
I guard the wild places.
Mountain, forest, and meadow.

I am the Lady in White
Lady of the mountains
Snow drifting down
Winter joy.

I am Guardian of Beasts
From the smallest mouse
To the largest bear.
Animals are sacred to me:
Revere them.

I am the old crone.
Wise woman
Shaman, Healer
Lady of herbs.

I bless you this season
As I ride across the sky
In my wild hunt
Hounds at my side.

Berchta: Ancient Alpine Goddess
Otherworldly Oracle[4]

Berchta: Goddess with Ancient, Mysterious Origins

Berchta is a name that's changed often over the centuries. A once widespread and greatly loved Germanic **goddess**, she still survives in German, Swiss, and Austrian folklore but under a different, more hideous guise. She is the leader of the Perchten. She is also known by Berhta, Bertha, Beraht, Perchta, Percht, Frau Percht, Frau Faste, Pehta, Perhta-Baba, and more. Berchta's origins are ancient Germanic; however, one theory suggests she was worshiped by ancient alpine Celtic tribes before the Germanic tribes. In his book Teutonic Mythology, Grimm writes of Berchta's cult centered in Southern Germany near the Black Forest, through the Alps of Switzerland, into Austria, the Czech Republic, Slovakia, and into France and Northern Italy, before the rise of the Church.

Berchta's Origins

She is likely much older as Grimm theorizes, because her attributes are seen in multiple goddesses throughout Europe. One specific Germanic goddess seems to be the same deity – Hulda (also known Huldra, Holda or Frau Holle). She is the Northern German aspect of Berchta (which we will explore later in this article). Berchta is associated with the ancient fertility goddess Nerthus, the Wild Hunt god Berchtold, and with Wodan (Germanic form of Odin). She might have been the same deity as Diana, Hecate, Abundia, or the Italian Christmas witch La Befana. Her name is still uttered at the Perchten parades in modern times.

---

[4] © 2020 Otherworldly Oracle, https://otherworldlyoracle.com/berchta-goddess-women-children-perchten/

Berchta: Goddess, Psychopomp, Shapeshifter

Berchta was a beloved goddess who protected babies, children, and women. Through Grimm's writings, we see glimpses into a past Germany where Berchta was a psychopomp (a guide to the afterlife), caring especially for babies and children's souls. Gently, like a mother, she leads them to the next life. In one tale of Berchta, in which a grieving mother spots her recently-deceased little boy following a group of children along a hillside. The children are following a motherly woman in a white gown. The boy breaks away to address his sorrowful mother. In his hands he shows her a bucket of water, which he says is his mother's tears. Then he tells her not to weep for him, for he is safe and sound under the White Lady's watch (Berchta).

Berchta's Three Keys

Because of her association with the cycle of life-death-rebirth, Berchta wears a belt with three golden keys hanging from it. The three keys represent the three cycles: birth/death/rebirth of which Berchta presides over. She had long, black hair worn in braids on the sides of her head, and wears a long, white gown. This is why she has been referred to as the White Woman or Lady in White, etc. In later tales, Berchta appears as a hag or crone, an elderly woman in disheveled dress. This could indicate Berchta as a triple goddess—maiden, mother, and crone, or it demonstrates the demonization of her name with the rise of the Church.

Shapeshifter

Another major aspect of Berchta is her shapeshifting abilities. Berchta has been described as having the feet of a goose or one goose-foot. She also takes the form of a swan. This indicates another of her attributes involved protection of wildlife, but it also recognizes Berchta as a shapeshifter. This isn't a far-fetched idea, since many of the ancient gods and goddesses were connected with the animal-world and were shapeshifters or deified land spirits. In this regard, Berchta was the "guardian of beasts".

Birch and Evergreens

From my research in Germanic folklore and mythology, Berchta's name is derived from the word *birch*, as in the *birch* tree. Berchta has a deep connection with the birch tree, which was a well-known representation of the goddess in Scandinavia. The rune Berkano is named for the birch tree, and is directly related to the goddess' name Berchta, therefore this rune is sacred to Berchta.

Other Sacred Plants

Because Berchta was an alpine goddess, she lives under the evergreen trees and the holly tree is sacred to her. Other plants in her domain include mayflower (which she holds in her hand in some spring lore), flax (which she spins along with people's fate), wild berries and, as mentioned previously, birch trees. Animals associated with Berchta include the goose, swan, mountain goat, cricket, owl, and fox. Any animal in the Alpine region is under her domain and protection (ibex, weasel, marmot, stork, etc). Berchta's home is the mountains.

Berchta in Folklore

After the Church's rise to power in the Middle Ages, Berchta became less and less god-like. She was no longer worshiped as she had been before. Because of her widespread cult, the Church had no other option but to demonize her. They demoted her from a Goddess to a witch. Her name became a fairy tale ... a piece of folklore ... a name to be feared.

The Wild Hunt

One well-known legend in Europe is the Wild Hunt. The Wild Hunt is a procession of spirits, witches, and demons that ride through the skies on certain nights of the year, collecting the souls of the dead. Some tales say these are the souls of the recently deceased, others say they were fairies or devils. Berchta became one of the Wild Hunt spirits. In most tales, she became a leader of the Wild Hunt alongside Wotan or Berchtold.

God Procession and Christmas Witches

The Wild Hunt was derived from an old pagan belief in god procession. The ancient pagan gods rode their horses in the clouds, either waging war or bringing abundance. On a side note, Odin is an early inspiration for Santa Claus as he was said to ride through the air on his steed – Sleipnir. And if we compare Berchta to the Italian Christmas Witch, La Befana, both rode through the air during the Christmas season bringing abundance. Also, if we think about Berchta as a psychopomp (guide to the dead), it makes sense why she was a part of the Wild Hunt, sweeping up the souls of the departed. The Wild Hunt might've become the Perchten.

Berchta and Holda

Berchta is another version of the Germanic goddess Holda. When Holda is mentioned in German folklore, her name is often substituted with Berchta, and vice versa. When the writer inquired from a modern day German about Berchta, she confirmed Berchta is still a part of their traditions. Berchta or "Frau Berchta" or "Frau Holle" shakes out her feather bed, creating the first snow fall each year in Germany (sketch of Frau Holle shaking out her pillow can be seen below). In Grimm's Fairy Tales, there is a tale of Mother Holle. Mother Holle is a "fairy godmother" being who either punishes or bestows gifts on young women depending on their honesty and work ethic. This fairy tale relates to older Middle Age tales of Berchta leaving every-day items as a reward, such as wood-chips, which turn to gold for good, hard-working people.

Berchtentag and Berchtesgaden

Berchta's name is seen in two instances in modern Germany: Berchtentag, which is the Night of the Epiphany, and Berchtesgaden, a national park whose name translates to Berchta's Garden. Berchtentag, also known as the Night of the Epiphany, is commemorated on January 5th or 6th, and is the twelfth night of Christmas. Berchta visited families on Berchtentag, and it was encouraged to leave out fish and gruel, cakes and milk, as offerings else Berchta punish in gruesome ways. How closely does the tradition of modern-day Santa Claus, leaving cookies and milk on Christmas Eve, resemble the ancient tradition of leaving offerings for the gods?

Berchtesgaden is a town in the shadow of the German Bavarian Alps. Scholars debate on the etymology of the town's name; however, the writer believes the terms origins are clear— Berchta's Garden. It is a beautiful landscape with green forests, tall snow-capped mountains, and is known for its local salt mines which have economically enriched the town since the fifteen hundreds. Grimm mentions salt mines were associated with witches, therefore associated with Berchta. In modern times, Berchta's horde parades around Berchtesgaden to scare away the winter ghosts.

Mother Goose

Have you ever wondered where the story of Mother Goose came from? Some believe Mother Goose is a modern version of Mother Berchta. Berchta was flanked by geese, and her counterpart Holda is wears a goose-down cape. Berchta shakes out her goose-down blankets to create the first snow each year. She has goose feet or one large goose-foot in many tales. Because she is a guardian of children, a guide of babies' souls in the afterlife, the good memory was passed down in the form of an old woman who kept children's stories alive...in the form of Mother Goose. If we examine the modern depictions of Berchta, Frau Holle, etc. there is an uncanny resemblance to Mother Goose.

A Demonized Berchta and the Perchten

Unfortunately, Berchta as the White Lady, gift-giver, guide and protector of babes, domestic goddess of spinning and women, was nearly stomped out when the Church rose to power. When the Church came against pagan customs that couldn't be absorbed, the only way to get the "pagans" to convert was to use fear. So Berchta, the wise white lady, was demonized and turned into a crooked-nosed, belly-slitting witch and leader of the Perchten. There were tales of Berchta the witch who captured children and ate them, similar to the horrific tales of Krampus. There were tales of Berchta, the Christmas hag, who would stuff the bad kids into her giant sack. If she was displeased with her offerings on the Night of the Epiphany, she would slit the person's belly open and stuff him or her with straw. Berchta's ancient link to the Winter Solstice wouldn't be snuffed out, so the Church had to frighten the new converts into believing she was a demon. An iron-nosed, hideous hag who would eat babies and mutilate people. This isn't a theory. It's a fact. The cult of Berchta was outlawed in Bavaria (where Berchtesgaden is located) in the year of 1468, according to the Thesaurus Pauperum. Leaving Berchta offerings during Christmas-time was also forbade and documented by church officials in the same century.

The Perchten

In addition to Berchta becoming a frightening Christmas belly-slitting witch, her consorts became terrifying demons—the Perchten. A tradition of dressing in hideous masks and taking part in parades around the Christmas holidays still happens in modern times in Germany (in Berchtesgaden), Switzerland, Austria, etc. The Perchten parade alongside Krampus, and the people belive it's an old folk tradition to scare away the winter ghosts. The Perchten scare away more than ghosts!

Berchta, The Belly Slitter

The terrifying names of Berchta—the iron-nosed and the belly-slitter—while a part of her demonization, show an ancient shamanic tradition of initiation. What struck me as intriguing is Berchta's act of slitting bellies and filling them with straw. Shamanic initiation involves the shaman going through a near-death experience, often with visions of losing limbs or being disemboweled, and then being "put back together" again. What the Church called "bad" people were people who rebelled or stuck with their original customs, and therefore Berchta would "slit their bellies". Sounds scary but to ancient pagans was a wink to shamanic initiation. As far as her iron-nose, there's a clear correlation with other ancient goddesses who were demonized, including the well-known Hungarian hag, the iron-nosed Baba Yaga (it should be noted this forest-witch sat at a spinning wheel and lived in a house atop a large bird foot).

Berchta's Beauty Remains

If we view Berchta as the demonized, child-eating witch, then we are still keeping her name alive. But if we were to really dive into the depths of her name, her ancestral lineage, and beautiful history, we would see she is much different than modern church and folkloric distinctions portray. She didn't eat children, she protected and guided them. She punished those who deserved punishment, but rewarded those were pure of heart. Her beauty and light can be seen in the wild and snow-capped peaks of the Alps to this day.

Perchta, My Teacher

Heather Rohan Choppin

Mountains High
Wild Pines
Aromatic sap
Fills the Air.
Wilderness solitude
Makes my heart
Rejoice.
Chitter chatter of
Red squirrels,
My Spirit Soars.
Distant Light
Beckons Me
Campfire Burns.
Smokey smell
Brings Comfort
Relax Here.
Distant Drumming
Grows louder
Until it is deafening.
I open my eyes
Before me a
Wise Woman
Ancient yet Strong.
Shaman Teacher
Dressed in wool
And furs. Colorful
Strips of cloth
Dance in the breeze
Like ribbons.
Become the Fire
She tells me.
I dance around

The Fire. Faster and
Faster until I
Merge and become one.
I see many things
Many pasts
Burned to ash
And Possible
Futures. Become
Phoenix.
I am Fire!

Lady of Hounds

Frodo, as dictated to Heather Rohan Choppin

My name is Frodo. My brother is named Pippin, also known as "Fool of a Took". Our mother is a huge "Lord of the Rings" fan, if you still can't tell. I am a very energetic and social whippet Labrador retriever mix who loves going on adventures. I love traveling with my head out the window and meeting every person or animal I see. Human disease (Covid-19) spreading is ruining my life. Mom won't let me interact with anyone outside our pack and we don't go traveling anymore. No dog parks, no meeting new animals, no meeting new humans, no dog play dates, no visiting pet stores, no dog parades, it's made me so depressed. My theme song is "Bored in the House" by Curtis Roach.

Every year I have many shots to keep me healthy including canine influenza or kennel cough. (Note from mom: doggo flu shot is like it is for people. Only a few strains are covered in the shot, while hundreds of flu germs exist. A dog can still get another flu virus, causing kennel cough.) Two days after coming home from daycare I started to get a deep-chested cough. Mom knew immediately what was wrong with me, and talked to the vet and got some over the counter medicine. The medicine was to keep me going for the two to six weeks I suffered from this cough. I was miserable all night.

Momma prayed to Holda and gave her an offering asking her to help heal us since Holda also has doggos of her own. "Grandma" Holda told mom to get us elderberry syrup, even though the vet did not suggest that option. Mom listens well and went to the magical place food comes from (store) and got me medicine. I licked it out the cup before bed and it tasted yummy. I slept all night snuggled up against momma under the covers. I woke up the next day with only a few coughs and by the day after I was all well. But I gave the virus to Pippin, so he started coughing, and Mommy did the same with Pippin that she did with me. "Grandma" Holda helped heal us with her magical syrup almost overnight when we should have been sick for weeks. She is a healing goddess in her own way and she loves her hounds and all doggos.

Holda's Rites

An Altar for Holda

Shannon Graves

Holda's altar should be in the kitchen, if possible. Find a shelf for her to stay on. The following items are all possibilities:

- A handmade linen altar cloth, handwoven or hand-embroidered, white and blue.
- A small model of a cottage.
- White feathers.
- Winter decorations, such as snowflakes or icicles. Christmas ornaments work well here.
- Drop spindles and small spinning wheels.
- Dried elderflowers or elderberry syrup.
- Brooms, from tiny to large.
- Flaxseed.
- Linen thread.
- Small livestock animals.
- A miniature wagon.
- Little elf figurines for the Huldrefolk.
- Recipe books.
- Cleaning supplies—keep these under the altar to be blessed.

Holda Housecleaning Rite

Shannon Graves

This is not a ritual for just "cleaning the house" as it is a ritual for finding motivation to clean the house. It's said that the goddess Holda punished lazy housekeepers, and it's true that for many of us, it takes a huge amount of effort just to get started, much less keeping up with it. This ritual is the one that you do when the mess gets huge and feels overwhelming, and you don't think that you can handle it. Holda is the one to call on, not because she isn't ruthless, but because she is.

First, kneel in the worst part of the mess. If you need to sweep away bits of it in order to do so, that's all right. Put your hands on the floor (or the horrid carpet, or whatever) and say to her:

Stiffen my spine that I might sweep
The grime from ground and garden.
Sharpen my sight that I might see
The way through mess and muddle.
Strengthen my will that I might wash away
Disarray and disorder from door to door.

Then stand and go to the hearth of the home—usually the kitchen where the stove pilot light burns, but if you've got a fireplace in your living room and you feel that's the real hearth, go for it. Lay out a piece of bread with butter, and a cup of tea (any kind) on top of one flawless white napkin. Light some scented herbs for incense (not on the napkin); culinary ones are best for Holda. I use kitchen sage, thyme, dill seed, and various spices on a lit charcoal disc. Blow the smoke around the room and say to her:

Hail Holda, healer of house and hearth,
As I feed you, so may you feed me

On soup of strength and meat of might,
On pottage of purpose and perseverance,
Hold me up to face this task
And fail me not, nor let me fail.

Then pick up a broom and sweep for a few minutes. It doesn't matter if there's carpet on the floor and the broom isn't going to do anything. Just sweep, because it invokes Holda's energy into the room. Lift the broom in the air and walk around the mess, waving it. As it waves, the mess should become less frightening. When you've done that for a few minutes, put on some loud music and start cleaning. It will be easier than you think—and when it becomes difficult, you'll feel Holda holding you up and keeping you on track.

Lessons From the Lady of the Look
Brandon E. Hardy

When I learned about Holda, I had already become taken with devotional cleaning. In fact, getting to clean altars and places of worship was the first type of cleaning I had ever enjoyed. It was after meeting my spiritual teacher and extending this joy to cleaning his kitchen that I met Her. My teacher showed me the small altar sitting next to his woodburning stove and spoke of Holda, sharing some of Her stories and names.

But personally, I began to call Her the Goddess of the Silent and Knowing Look. Whenever I collapsed into the rocking chair in the corner for a break from cleaning the kitchen, Her figurine was always staring at me. Very directly. It didn't matter how I positioned Her idol earlier that day. It also didn't matter how I rearranged Her altar to help prevent this. I would slump down to rest and look up to meet Her gaze. It became a reminder that She was watching, and that I could do better ... or at least work harder. She wasn't wrong, and when I was cleaning for my teacher, I began also making these efforts an offering to Her. It wasn't long before another altar to Her was forming in my room. When I took my vows, it was She who spoke down my ancestral line to give me my new name.

Fast-forward a few years to when I found myself by my bed praying, on my knees and almost in tears. It was directed to Whoever was listening and willing to answer. There was so much chaos happening around me, my depression was helpfully responding by worsening, and I felt entirely lost. I wanted clarity in my confusion; everything I tried changed nothing. That's when I got my answer from Holda.

Sometimes I get to experience the sensation of a response to a prayer as if it were settling in my heart, much like the emotions that come with a sentiment rather than the words of the sentiment itself. That works its way through my personal filter to become an "answer"... with a large allowance for human error. To date, the response that comes through the most is an unsatisfying reminder that I have an anxiety disorder and could probably use a nap. With Holda, I had never experienced more than that Silent, Knowing Look, the one that meant we both knew perfectly well what I should be doing, and that I wasn't doing it. But while this answer was a change of style for Her, it really wasn't that different from the usual.

"Have you tried cleaning your room?"

I was somewhat taken aback. Not only by the Who, but because seriously, what kind of answer was that? I was having a crisis! If I cleaned my room, what good would that do for all of the emotional crap happening both inside and outside of it? My spiritual path wouldn't suddenly have direction because I folded my socks! I put my head back down and clarified my interest in a slightly more existential answer. She let Her opinion on that be summarized by a resounding silence.

Then I took a good look around myself at my living space... and found it to be an obnoxiously accurate mirror for my mental state. It showed as many signs of depression as my behaviors did. It was just as cluttered, confused, and stagnant as my mind and actions, with an overwhelming theme of being so clogged that nothing had space to move forward.

The room was still an improvement from what I was used to when I was growing up. A friend once described my room by saying that if I ever snapped and killed someone, the police would take one look at it and arrest me. I had been building systems to better cope with my ADHD, including my beloved "things I most commonly forget when walking out the door then have to come back for" drawer and countless rounds of dealing with the backlog of my hoarding habits. That book "The Life Changing Magic of Tidying Up" stalked me in a distressingly persistent way for a few years until I compromised and got its sequel "Spark Joy". (It had a lot more pictures. Far less overwhelming.) I had been reading that and pacing myself through creating a more tidy situation. The improvement had been remarkable ... until a couple months before I had found myself kneeling to pray in the pile of dirty laundry by my bed.

Being there on the floor among it all, that's when I could see what to do. Turning it from purely self-help into a semi-devotional task cut through my fog. People who are familiar with magic should know the phrase "as above, so below", but Holda seemed much more focused on the inverse, "as below, so above". So I decided to start working on the "below", with the intent of my mind becoming as orderly as my room. It was many weeks of dicking around and trying to make it past unhelpful neurology, pain, and continuing depression until I finally reached the milestone I had been envisioning for years. There were still projects left incomplete, boxes of stuff in the extension waiting to leave, and the storage portion of my closet was left in its semi-sorted state, but my space was tidied and easily accessible. Clothes were all folded and put away. Every item shoved in a corner had found a proper place. The drawers and shelves of craft supplies were not only functional, but sorted. It was no longer the refuge of a childhood me insulating from both internal and external chaos, but a space for who I was and needed to be now.

A few weeks later I was chatting with a childhood friend who has similar cleaning struggles to myself, so I offered to show her some of the sorting tricks I had learned or figured out that kept the act from entirely wrecking me. These were mostly small tidbits of advice paired with much pointless enthusing. (Did I mention I have ADHD?) I started trying to explain how it had helped me improve parts of my life on a more spiritual level, but I couldn't quite get all my thoughts in order. And this annoyed me, so the next day I jotted down a few bullet points. Then as more popped up I would add those to the list, until it was much longer than I had expected. What had come out as a few disorganized ideas the night previous was now a massive jumble of half-formed sentences.

Later, while trying to read what I had scribbled down so I could translate it for people outside of my head, I noticed something weirdly familiar. One part of the cleaning practice looked like a technique I had been struggling with in Buddhist-style meditation for quite a while. (Well, less like "struggling with" and more like "avoiding entirely".) Then as I reread the rest of the notes through this new lens, more similarities started popping up. Every coping mechanism I had used to deal with cleaning that space had in turn honed a skill I could begin to use on my own mind, the very mind that had manifested in that clutter with a painful amount of accuracy. The "full circle" of it all was very satisfying.

I went to work turning those scribbles into full sentences, hoping I could express this skillset that had literally made the ephemeral into something tangible; that had made the "above" a bit more "below". Then in turn, maybe I could figure out how to go back the other way, using the tangible to work on those ephemeral bits that I wasn't great at. And if there's anything I'm not great at, it's meditation.

The first step often given for Buddhist meditation is to simply practice. Sit silently. Focus on the breath. Power through, but without powering through. This can be miserable for a beginner; I know that it certainly has been for me. While the issues that interfered when I was younger are no longer as much of a concern, I've now hit other health-related stumbling blocks while trying to find that stillness. Since any possible benefits of quietly sitting were being promised in the long term, I was not finding the motivation to stick through the physical discomfort and neurological restlessness.

Moving meditations were offered as alternatives, especially walking meditations. I actually enjoy these a great deal and have had much success in pursuing them, but I felt like I was developing a different set of skills. It helped me reach a beneficial state of mind while on the move, but when it came to being at peace with where I was, it just didn't seem to translate. And when movement isn't always an option in a very literal way, that matters. Cleaning with Holda became what I needed to bridge the gap between movement and stillness. The quieting of the chaos of my room quieted the swirling inside me, too. Using that lovely power of 20/20 hindsight, here's a bit of what I think was happening.

Making It Tangible

Organizing my room was (and is) a significantly more straightforward experience for me than doing the same for the amorphous blob that was (and is) my mind. This simple concept is a connecting thread through every part of this practice. I already mentioned how Holda flipped the saying into "as below, so above", and these practices take shape in that "below". While cleaning and organizing is still a struggle, I have enough experience with my physical body to make starting out here easier than when working in the "above". I understand how to use my eyes to look at my room, even if it took me time to learn how to process what I was looking at. The same goes for my hands, that I only had to worry about what to pick up and where it should be put down, as I already knew how to handle the limitations of my grip. The tools of this type of magic are far more familiar to me.

In addition, even small improvements from my efforts were easily noticeable, as were changes in the flow of day-to-day life. Being able to easily grab my wallet on the way out the door or knowing where to find my nail clippers sounds unremarkable in the Grand Scheme of Spirituality, yet seeing once unattainable goals in my life become commonplace gave me the hope needed to spark motivation around this other unattainable practice. (It also reduces stress quite a bit to lose things less often, and that just helps everything.)

Now I have a hold on what the anxiety and frustration that comes before this kind of success can feel like, and view it as a step rather than immediately as a sign that I'm doing something wrong or impossible in my meditation. That also goes for when I simply have one of those bad days where all the systems I created aren't working and it feels like I haven't made any progress at all. Being able to note my stress responses on these low-functioning days creates a framework for the days that meditation is more difficult. Just because the back pain this week results in me putting off laundry doesn't mean every improvement in hamper management is lost, and just because the same back pain also means I can't sit quietly for more than thirty seconds doesn't mean I won't be back to longer meditation in a few days. The same concept applies when the inside of my head is a screaming blender. The results of making some peace with my physical world have become both a literal and figurative example of how I can view the struggles of my meditative life.

Being Willing to Face My Bullshit

But to do any practice, one has to have a good idea of what they're working with. This means getting at least some grasp of one's current state before any steps can be made towards change. It's like that saying about leading a horse to water ... except when I ended up at the water I would always get distracted by how distasteful I found my own reflection on the surface. To be able to drink, I was going to have to give that face a kiss.

This has to be paired with initiative, because looking at this stuff sucks. There was a reason this mess was happening in the first place. The pitfalls of doing nothing had to outweigh the coping mechanism enough that I would be able to truly stare myself in the eye. I also had to accept that sometimes the desire to strive towards a goal wasn't going to be enough to push me through my depression and discomfort. So as I once read it summarized quite beautifully: "True change only happens when I'm tired of my own bullshit." And I had become really, really tired. Letting myself acknowledge fully how done I was with the way I was existing gave me something to fill in for the times I didn't feel worthy of the goals I wanted to reach, or when the whole thing just felt too overwhelming.

To be able to truly create change in my living space, I had to face down the shame I held about being the type of person who would let things reach this point. Instead of turning away from every now-grimy food container or stack of stressfully unsorted belongings, I had to see them and own that I had done that. And not just own it, but give space for it, which is where practicing "non-judgment" of myself often broke down. But the initiative and bullshit-exhaustion pushed me through, and eventually I found tricks for my own mental barriers that helped calm the internal swirl enough to make decisions. I did a lot of facing down my anxiety, reclaiming the opinions of myself that I found there, then breaking down the illogical thought patterns that kept me frozen. Through the cracks so created sprouted the opportunities for realistic troubleshooting.

A good starting point was my habits around clothing. When I find myself free to strip naked and collapse into bed, my clothes rarely find themselves sorted into the laundry or put back away where they might stay clean. They instead ended up on the eternally dusty unfinished wood floor, filling in for the sweeping I was avoiding. To deal with this, I had to face realities that I didn't like looking at. I had to see the limitations of my neurology and my body, and that meant accepting how extremely difficult it could be to mentally process how to sort clothes, or even have the fine motor skills needed to handle them. What I felt was something simple that I should "just be able to do" was embarrassingly hard for me. I needed to treat this difficulty not as a failure from which to avert my eyes, but neutrally as one of the many realities of my reflection. More specifically, I needed to stop planning for the way I thought I should be or who I wish I was, and instead plan for who I was right then. So I decided on a place where I could toss my clothes on the days I just couldn't deal and built a routine for sorting them when I was capable. What was once a shame-filled task steeped in intense anxiety and a pervading sense of hopelessness became a solution with clear directions, then eventually a happy success.

This became another framework for meditation, but this time for identifying the skin-crawling feeling when I was starting to face down parts of myself that made me cringe. The feelings that cropped up while truly facing down my living space were the same that happened when truly facing down myself, and in both instances it instinctually had me turning away. But while I could delude myself into thinking that there was nothing in that particular spot of my mind to look at, I couldn't delude myself into thinking that my laundry was being handled well when I had to step on a pile of it to get out of bed. I could ignore it or pretend it wasn't that big of a deal, but I was definitely having the visceral experience of wading through laundry.

So I had to be present. I had to come out of my avoidant haze and be there with the laundry piles of my brain. By doing this, the detached emotional observance of meditation went from feeling like dissociation to instead a tool of acceptance. By not overreacting, I could start gathering mental laundry and figure out what to do about it.

Small Steps

One of the most wonderful things that I took away from an ADHD self-help program was the concept of breaking big, overwhelming tasks down into smaller and smaller parts until each step inspired the least amount of anxiety possible. When facing down the idea of being a more tidy person, the idea of organizing my whole room was overwhelming, so I focused on creating a small foundation and building from there. If I didn't have the patience for facing all the issues in my life, could I have patience for just dealing with my bedroom? If not, then perhaps I could go through that one insistently constant pile of belongings on my floor? If not, could I just take one book from the pile and put it on the bookshelf? A bit nearer to the bookshelf? While the manual I was using for "tidying up" suggested doing it all at once, and that is something I had success with in full overhaul situations, at this point I was trying to build routines that would be part of day-to-day life. Accidentally ending up with a large amount of clutter was a quality of myself I was learning to accept would always be there, so I had to figure out how to live with it while not constantly making the cleaning of it an overhaul-level event.

This meant I began tangibly experiencing the domino effect that could be started by making one small, yet relatively solid, healthy change in my life. For instance, troubleshooting how to keep better track of my wallet (having a designated drawer space for it to live in, getting a bigger wallet to make its presence—or lack thereof—more noticeable, etc.) then led to a drawer for storing it and other important leaving-the-house items, which lead to figuring out a system I could use for these items when traveling for months at a time. Now that I have this notable proof of improvement (among many others), what I once considered to be dismissible small behavior changes are viewed with far more appreciation.

When facing down the overwhelming concept that is Meditation, already having the habit of identifying these stacking small accomplishments in self-improvement is incredibly beneficial. When the first bits of depression or anxiety show up, asking, "Why should you even bother?" or "Are you even doing this right?", these bits of proof, small as they may be, might just change the answer. Or maybe your mental health has upended your life again and now you find yourself trying to restart. Having an idea of how to watch those bits stack back up again can help curb at least some of the frustration at having to rebuild.

Setting Reasonable Goals

Like I mentioned before, I'm just messy by nature. As I've built up and adjusted my cleaning practices over the years, I've had to accept this. A certain amount of cluttering happens if I don't stay vigilant, be it from health flares, mental issues, or straight up laziness. I call this "silting". It means there are no actual issues with the cleaning structure I've established, I just haven't put much effort into keeping the flow going lately, so clutter is starting to collect. Sometimes there's a chronic problem that's worth troubleshooting, and a bit of reorganizing here or there is simply part of normal maintenance. Sometimes a good chunk of reorganizing is needed as my space doesn't function too well when it gets overly static, and letting it "breathe" helps keep that flow moving.

But I've found there's a point where spending all that effort on cleaning starts to become its own issue. There's a difference between "being functional" and "perfectly cleaning everything", especially when I'm being realistic about the amount of work it takes me to reach "functional". After a certain point, pushing forward begins to feel like cleaning for the sake of cleaning, like I'm treating this "silting" as more than it actually is. While I'm enjoying the process of it all, it's usually a sign that I have lost sight of why I'm cleaning in the first place. It's certainly not to achieve some sort of level of precision and perfection, because that's not only unrealistic, but ultimately self-destructive when I continually fall short. It's supposed to be to create a healthy, functional situation for who I am and what I want to do. It's so I can treat my living space and belongings with gratitude and respect. It's so I can continue to learn from my own struggles, and from that place honor the struggles of others.

And that connects right back to meditation. While the degree may vary, my mind is always going to be a bit of a mess. Whether it's from the side-effects of chronic pain, neurology, trauma, or simply good old madness, it's unreasonable to hold myself to standards of mental "perfection" that are unattainable. And things are even going to "silt" up in my head as much as they do in my living space, so I just need remember what I'm doing and why I'm doing it. I need to keep on it as I am able, accept my periods of what feels like relapse, respect the body I find myself in, and do my best to avoid responding with destructive extremes. There's a comfortable ground in-between somewhere that is a far better place for me to work towards. Buddhism's not called "the Middle Way" for nothing!

Mess Divination

After doing Holda's "as below, so above" practice for some time, I started noticing patterns in the way my clutter would accumulate. If I was having issues around motivating myself to do art, I would notice that things had been starting to "silt" between my bed and my art supplies for days. If I was having trouble connecting with a certain deity, I would find that something I had forgotten on the floor was blocking me from being able to comfortably reach Their altar.

It got to the point that I would just stand in my room and look around to see where messes had formed. From there I could identify where blockages were also forming in my interior blind spots before they made themselves more loudly known. Much like a diviner throwing down bones or rocks and reading the results, I was looking at the clothes, dishes, and forgotten projects I had blindly tossed down. There will always be a level of chaos in my living space, so it's unreasonable to expect my surroundings to be any more static than my mind. And just as my internal chaos can leave space for messages to slip through, my external chaos can sometimes lead to that as well. The Gods are very skilled at working with what we have to offer. Cleaning up those types of messes became a segment of time I could spend on the corresponding area in myself.

There's also a difference between this "mess divination" and an unkempt altar. I think of the latter like "leaving a mess in Their space and Them being reasonably displeased", which is different from "there's a mess inside of my space (both physically and mentally) and that's keeping me from being open to Them". Insulating from the intensity of that kind of connection, no matter how it happens, is natural. And it's important to take steps to address it.

More than once I've had it expressed to me that prayer is like "speaking", while meditation is more like "listening". So just as meditation can help open oneself up to "listening" more fully, prolonged practice of this cleaning with Holda gave me a way to do it as well. Not only does it show me where I was resisting hearing something, but it also gives me a way to address and lessen that resistance. Then by the time I sit down to meditate, the blocks that made the listening in my day-to-day spiritual life uncomfortable have already been lessened. And by being able to identify where those feelings of lessening are happening in me, I can also pay those blocked areas special attention when trying to deepen my meditation.

These are the foundations of what She showed me. Maybe some of it has rung true to your situation, maybe some of it gives you an idea of how to move forward, or maybe you somehow stuck through to the end only to be disappointed. Whichever of those it was, I'm hoping you also made it to this point because you are searching for a way to deal with your own messes, because it's in the spirit of that which I feel the need to make one more point.

As much as I tie all of this back to Buddhist meditation, the cleaning I was doing with Holda was manifesting in its own time and way. It translates to meditation, but something can only be translated when it's a language in its own right. What Holda taught me was a form of magic. Yet when I explain what happened step-by-step, it sounds incredibly practical and mundane. That's because it is. That's where I find so many of Her blessings, and it's what I hope She will bring you as well during your own journey. May She show you the magic in the practical and the mundane, then grant you the fortitude and clarity to do something with it.

Cooking With Holda

Raven Kaldera

Throughout much of my life, I'd decided that I hated cooking. I could make a box of food for my child when she was young, if needed, but my single-parenting was sadly lacking in home-cooked food. Fortunately, I always seemed to have partners and/or housemates who could cook better than I could, and were willing to feed myself and my child if I funded the ingredients. That was a great solution for a long time ... as long as we were eating the same food.

My blockage around cooking came from an abusive childhood where I was forced to do nearly all the housework for a family variously burdened with physical, mental, and neurological illnesses. Where other children went to their friends' houses after school, I was kept under virtual house arrest and made to keep the house clean and look after my younger sister, and was beaten if I slacked off and did it wrong. I knew that if I showed any aptitude for cooking, I would get stuck with that as well, so I rebelled and screwed up every time I was pushed to make food more complicated than a sandwich. It became a running joke in the family that I would "burn water", and I was just fine with that. Instead, I spent my childhood eating my sullen, depressed, angry mother's awful cooking which tasted of her roiling moods.

As an adult, I lived with hippies and bohemian housemates who were erratic cleaners at best, and didn't mind if I spent a decade indulging rebellion against daily cleaning, although I would take part in monthly clean-days when the mess became unmanageable. I was still lucky, though, in that there were folks willing to cook for me so that I didn't have to do it, so long as I bought the groceries. By the time I was on my second marriage—with a spouse far messier that I'd ever been, but who could cook!—I'd settled into a pattern of permanent rebellion.

Eventually, though, I got over it. I had my own home by then, and while I do suffer from chronic illness which often makes it difficult to do any kind of physical work, I learned how cleaning can be a magical cleansing charm for your soul. As you do the dishes, you announce that you are also cleaning yourself—cleaning out all the silted-up gunk of the day, the week, the month's pains and annoyances. I did feel better afterwards, and I had a clean area to gaze upon proudly.

Cooking, however, took longer to come around to. By then I had a file of recipes for fancy party foods, which I could make to impress people once in a while—the baking equivalent of the guy who can barbecue on Sundays but wouldn't ever think of cooking the daily dinner. Then my health issues got drastically worse, thanks to my ongoing case of genetic lupus which continues to progress and affect everything in my body. I developed multiple allergies which slowly made eating premade food (or even the food made with "ordinary" ingredients by my partners and housemates) impossible. I developed diabetes, as I have three genetic disorders which all put me at risk—my bloodlines were against me. I also had a seizure disorder that was getting worse. I'd always had a fair amount of body hatred and bodily dissocation due to disability and gender dysphoria, and that affected my relationship with food. Eventually it became clear that I would have to start a permanently restricted diet to control as many of my health problems as possible—and that meant I would have to learn to take care of my own food.

For the first year of my heavily restricted diet, I had a gluten-free housemate who was willing to cook for me. That was a godsend to get me used to what really felt like deprivation (among other things, I'd had to quit a heavy sugar addiction entirely, and at the time I was allergic or sensitive to almost all the artificial sweeteners on the market). But eventually he moved on, and I was left to fend for myself.

It was Holda and the Vanic Gods who stepped forward to help me with my food issues. While Frey worked on my attitudes toward food and my body, and Njord worked on freeing the part of my soul which had been trapped into house-slavery so long ago, Holda looked at me sharply and said, "There's power in controlling your own nourishment, you know." That made my eyebrows go up. It had literally never occurred to me that learning to cook could be a source of more independence in my life.

So I began to cook with Holda. Fortunately, by this time the internet was full of food nerds with all sorts of dietary issues, doing experiments and posting recipes, and every allergy and intolerance was shared by someone out there who was working on a way to make donuts when you couldn't have half the traditional ingredients, including flour or sugar. (Watermelon seed protein flour. Really.) I tried recipe after recipe, battling appetite fatigue and lack of ability to stand for long. I slowly became skilled at making good food that didn't make me feel deprived. The first time I made my own organic pizza with a sunflower-seed-flour crust that I judged to be better than anything I could get in any restaurant I could afford, it was a milestone.

Holda stood over my shoulder. "Put love into that food as you're making it. Put wishes of good health into it."

"But no one is going to eat it but me," I protested. The other people in the house wanted nothing to do with my "weird food" when they could eat "real food", and some were on entirely different health diets for their own issues. Holda glared at me, and I subsided and tried hard to follow her orders. It brought home to me how little I valued my own body over the bodies of others. The fact that putting positive energy into food only eaten by myself seemed like a waste forced me to look how little importance I placed on myself as anything but a vessel for work. "Fine," Holda said, exasperated. "You'll be a better vessel if you're healthier. Just do it." So I did.

At some point I inherited a couple of antique copper pans, which I intended to hang on the wall as kitchen décor. "No," said Holda. "You're going to cook in those."

So I got them retinned, learned about copper cookware, and promptly got scared. "I could ruin this!"

"Then you'll be careful and mindful," Holda said. And, slowly, I learned. Friends who were cleaning out their houses (and, sadly, the houses of their dead grandparents) during the early part of the COVID lockdown sent me more copperware, and I found yet more online for very cheap which were quite serviceable when retinned. Now I have a large collection of … well, I can only call them my devotional pots and pans. They still scare me to cook on, and I don't use them on bad days when I have few spoons and I'm likely to burn something and melt the tin into the food, but I'm learning.

I also got wooden spatulas and tongs to use with them, and when I take one down, wipe it off, and use it, Holda stands over my shoulder and gives me advice like a good grandmother.

I know that my own grandmother would had probably taught me some of this, had I ever gotten over my cooking-phobia before she died, and I am grateful for Holda standing in for her. I am, in my fifties, becoming some sort of kitchen witch, in the cooking sense. I am learning to work with the ingredients I have, cobbling good food out of strange bits, as I cobble useful days out of the stray bits of energy left to me.

Now I cook approximately every other day, give or take. My chronic illnesses still mean that I'm too sick sometimes, which is why I thriftily make more food than I can eat at any given time and freeze it. I boil down fishbones and other carcasses for broth and make soup, I've learned to poach fish and even made steamed pudding. I sing over the cooking food. I draw the rune Berkana, for growth and nurturing, in my alterna-piecrust. I've even learned how to make pseudo-ethnic food to sate my desire for the restaurants I can no longer visit—when you're allergic to soy and MSG, for example, any Asian restaurant is like playing Russian roulette. When I start to feel hemmed in by appetite fatigue, Holda says, "Try something new. There are a million combinations. Cooks throughout the ages often had to work with limited ingredients and still come up with something good. What can you make with what you have?"

After I use any piece of copper, I must immediately wash and dry it. There is no letting it sit around dirty, because that will encourage poisonous verdigris, which will mean polishing it. This means that the cookware itself has become an act which can be used to help me—"As I push myself to clean this pot, even though I am tired, may I also push myself to immediately treat my health problems as they arise, and not put them off until tomorrow."

A Swiss-born friend of mine once referred to cleaning with intent to cleanse yourself as the *Putzteufel* method—the word meant "cleaning devil", reminiscent of the kind of enthusiastic housekeepers Holda loves. I'm not a *Putzteufel* by any stretch of the imagination, but I can use the technique. That same friend left me my first Holda figurine when she passed on—a little corn dollie sitting at a spinning wheel. "To look after your house," she said. And she sits in the kitchen on her altar-shelf and watches over me, stands by my gleaming wall of copper and advises me, and cares. She cares. What more could I ask?

Twelve Days of Holda's Yule

Shannon Graves

Yule is the time of year most dedicated to Holda, and for those who want to quietly honour her, this can be done on each day throughout the season. On each of these days, you will make and eat one of her sacred foods.

- ❖ Dec. 21, Yule: When you wake up in the morning, pack up all fibre arts in the house, especially any spinning. Put them all in a nice box. Make an altar to Holda; you can check the link on this site to altar suggestions if you like. Put the box on the altar and ask her to bless it all. Put your hands palm down on the altar and ask her to bless them as well. The fibre arts should all stay on the altar until after the New Year. Next, go to the kitchen and make gingerbread cookies, dusted with powdered sugar like Holda's snowflakes.

- ❖ Dec. 22: Make oatmeal in the morning. Clean up after the Yule celebration. Sweep the house with a broom—for carpeted floors, do a symbolic sweeping and then actually vacuum. Open the window at the highest point, shake the broom out the window to drive out all negativity, and then ask Holda to bring happiness to your home.

- ❖ Dec. 23: Bake oatcakes. As you do so, ask Holda to bless the hearth.

- ❖ Dec. 24: Pickled herrings are on the menu—another of Holda's sacred foods. Clean the bathroom and ask Holda for her blessing to keep your house's waterways clear.

- ❖ Dec. 25: If you celebrate Christmas with relatives, as some Pagans do, make a white cake covered with frosting, for

Holda's snowy days. Give someone a gift of a new feather pillow.

- Dec. 26: Make some kind of dessert with elderberries—elderberry pie, or something involving elderberry jam. Organize the medicine cabinet and ask Holda for a healthy year.

- Dec. 27: Dumplings today, with or without soup. Use a bit of wintergreen oil in the wash water and mop the floors. As you do so, ask Holda for a clean year.

- Dec. 28: Bake biscuits with flaxseed in them. Do laundry, and put a drop of wintergreen oil in the wash water. Ask Holda to keep everyone clothed this year.

- Dec. 29: Make a dessert that looks like elf hats, or elfin food in some way. Put some of it out for the Huldrefolk, and ask Holda to keep things from mysteriously vanishing this year.

- Dec. 30: Bake more cookies with powdered sugar, such as pfeffernusse. Save half to eat during tomorrow night's celebrations. Clean the inside of the windows, and then place a candle in at least one window. Ask Holda to spare you from disastrous weather this winter.

- Dec. 31: Elderberry wine, as part of the New Year's Eve celebration. Ask Holda to keep everyone in the family safe, especially the mothers and children.

- Jan. 1: New Year's Day. This is a day of relaxation. Do nothing today except rest. Tomorrow, the fibre arts come out and the cleanup commences. Drink elderflower tea to regain your strength.

For the Hearth

Geordie Ingerson[5]

The hearth is the centre of the home, even if it is just a warm place in the kitchen, heated by a modern stove. Every modern stove has a pilot light, an ever-burning flame that can be blessed. Of course, if you are lucky enough to have a fireplace, or a modern wood-fired cooker or antique woodstove, you have a source of open flame that will be lighted on a regular basis. Lighting the hearth is a matter of calling on Mother Holda. I trace the fire-rune Ken in the ashes, and then light the fire, saying:

Holda, hold this hearth in your hand,
Make joyous all the hearts on this land,
Make warm the hopes that feel this fire,
Grant this home all it may require.

---

[5] All of Geordie Ingerson's charms previously appeared in his book, *Ingvi's Blessing: Spells and Charms for Field and Farm*, Asphodel Press, 2011.

For Elderflower Wine

Geordie Ingerson

Elder is the flower of Holda and so elderflower wine is drunk in her honour. (Elderberries are more the province of Hel, but elderflowers are like the snowflakes that Holda shakes from her goose-feather pillows.) Elder has a long history as a Pagan tree, being the last of the Celtic tree-months and considered the guardian of the road to Hel. It was called "the medicine-chest of the country people". Elder trees were treated like a living woman, and permission had to be asked before taking any of their flowers or berries. Later Christians disapproved of the regard given to the elder and called it the Devil's tree, and began a myth that Judas had hanged himself from it in order to make it a plant of ill omen.

In order to make elderflower wine, pick the flowers on a sunny day during their short growing season. Do not wash them; just shake the bugs off and pour four litres of boiling water over a pint of flowers and stems. Add the juice and grated rind of three organic lemons and 2 kilograms of sugar. When it has cooled to finger-warmth, add wine yeast and any yeast nutrient that you prefer. Cover it and leave it to ferment for three days. As soon as it is covered, say this prayer:

Flower of Holda, Lady of Home-Place,
Old woman of the bog and fen,
Give us your snow that falls in the summer
To warm us in winter again.

After three days, strain the mixture and put it into your brewing vessel. After two turns of the Moon the wine should be clear, and it is siphoned off into bottles. As the prayer says, wait until wintertime to drink it. You can make wine from a number of different flowers using this same method.

For Good Cooking

Geordie Ingerson

If you would have pots that never boil over or go dry, and baking that never burns, and food that is never overdone or underdone ... well, perhaps that is beyond the skill of any mortal. But you can come close to it with this prayer. Light a candle near the stove (if you can light it from the stove fire, all the better) and light a mugwort stick and wave smoke around the room. Then say:

Mother Holda who blesses the hearth,
I would have cauldrons that never boil over,
I would have food that never burns,
I would have all the spirits of the household
Work through my hands to feed my family
Only the best that can be made,
And waste nothing in the trial.
Grant me a sacred kitchen
And I shall be the keeper of this temple.

Of course, once you have made this prayer, you must keep the kitchen clean when not directly in use, as you would a temple. You should light smoke to propitiate the kitchen spirits regularly, and give them a portion of most of your meals.

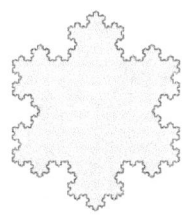

For Cleaning the Chimney

Geordie Ingerson

So long as there are chimneys there will have to be cleaning, so that creosote does not build up in them and present a fire hazard. These days, chimney cleaning is done with more modern tools and rarely does a sweep have to venture inside one—which is a good thing considering the cancer rates of chimney sweeps in the old days. The by-products of fire can be very dangerous. Similarly, the by-products of such fiery emotions as rage and smouldering resentments can build up a good deal of psychic creosote in the house as well, and the chimney cleaning is as good a time as any to remove such dangerous substances. As you work with brushes and (perhaps) vacuum cleaner, say the following prayer:

Mother Holda so quick with the broom,
Sharp eyes that catch all sloth and sulking,
Sweep us clean of all our resentments,
Sweep us clean of all our wrath,
Let the warmth of the hearth glow unencumbered
That we may all be family again.

For a Besom

Geordie Ingerson

It is not hard to make yourself a homemade broom. The handle is made with the straightest possible stick — in the past one of those coppiced saplings we spoke of earlier in this book. The broom is of birch twigs. Today they are tied on with wire, which pulls tighter than the traditional binding of willow withies. To make a traditional besom, one drills a hole through the end that will hold the broom and drives a wooden peg through it so that it protrudes about an inch on each side. Then the twigs are arranged around the handle and bound with flexible willow withies, above and below the peg so as to keep the bundle from slipping off.

The besom was the traditional witch's implement, but long before that the people went out in the unploughed fields in spring and danced to make the grain tall. They straddled besoms, shovels, rakes, and any other implement as a "steed", and the height that they and their steed could leap would be the grain's height for the year. Later, when such capering fertility rites had fallen violently out of favour, these antics were associated with witches, the Devil, and the use of hallucinogenic flying ointment. Witches were shown first flying with the broom-ends down to "sweep their tracks out of the sky", then with the broom-end up a century later, perhaps bearing a candle to light the way, then again with the broom-end fashionably lowered.

Brooms are still used as a symbol of fertility and many Pagan brides and bridegrooms jump over them at weddings to encourage abundance. They are also hung beside doorways in kitchens to invoke the domestic house spirits and make the kitchen a warm and comfortable place. While she is more of a Germanic goddess than a Scandinavian one, I associate the besom with Mother Holda and this prayer invokes her:

Steed of ancient fertile field,
Mother of ancient fertile home,
Holda's hunting horse that sweeps
All clean as we together waltz,
Bless our home with every stroke.

Blessing a New Basket

Geordie Ingerson

Baskets can be woven out of reed, willow, or splits of oak or ash—or, for that matter, all manner of saplings and twigs gathered from the land. The earliest container was probably some form of basket, made from perishable materials that we will never find. Man's need for containers, especially in the early nomadic days, was more important than his need for food—it is believed that the earliest cultivated plant was not some sort of grain but a bottle gourd for transporting food.

While weaving a basket, one can call on Mother Holda to bless it. The various items suggested in the charm can be replaced with what the basket is actually planned to hold, if anything.

By seed that springs up
And reaches for sky,
Thou shalt hold wool,
And thou shalt hold fruit.
Thou shalt be strong
And never betray me,
Thou shalt hold berries
And Holda hold thee.

For Spinning

Geordie Ingerson

Many legends have been built around Mother Holda and her penchant for spinning. She was said to punish lazy women who neglected their daily spinning and sewing, and to helpfully do the work of women who had collapsed exhausted by their spindles and wheels and looms and sewing baskets, taking up their work while they slept. (In general, she is said to reward the diligent and punish the slothful.) The ancient Norse women used spindles made of soapstone, which is easily carved and sanded into such shapes.

Spindles can be carved with runes depending on what sort of energy you wish to create while spinning, and that same energy will go into the thread and the cloth that is woven from it. A spinning wheel can be carved with the rune of your choice, but a good choice might be a Sowelu rune for the sun-wheel. While you spin, say (or even better, sing) this prayer:

Mother Holda, hands of power,
Fingers quick as flax-blue flower,
Make my thread spin fine and strong,
Ever soft and ever long,
With all the power borne in your song.

For Weaving

Geordie Ingerson

After the dyebath, we are back to the realm of Mother Holda again, and the thread is woven into cloth. We also call upon the Norns in this charm, the goddesses who weave all Wyrd. This charm is good to sing, one line at a time, as the shuttle goes through and the beater bangs against the weft.

As I weave you,
So I wish health,
So I wish wealth,
So I wish joy,
In the holy name
Of wise Dame Holda.
As I weave you,
So I will health,
So I will wealth,
So I will joy,
In the holy name
Of wise Dame Holda.
Hail to Urd,
Hail to Skuld,
Hail to Verdandi that weaves us all.

For Soapmaking

Geordie Ingerson

Soap has two ingredients: fat and lye. The fat can be animal fat or olive oil or glycerine; the lye can be store-bought or homemade. Other additives such as scents or abrasives are for personalizing the soap. Sacred soaps can be made for cleansing before any ritual, or simply to use in the name of a deity – goat milk soap could be for Thor, oatmeal soap for Frey, flower-scented soap for Freya, herb-scented soap for Gerda, and so on. However, the process is watched over by the cleaning goddess, Mother Holda, so when the soap is cooling in its pans, we pray:

Hail Holda whose broom cleanses all our woes,
Let your alchemy turn two evils to good,
Let this soap cleanse both body and soul.

Holda's Elderberry Potion

Mercy Karinczy

Elderberries can often be found growing wild along the road—their sprays of tiny purple-black berries are pretty obvious. In Europe, they are small trees (*Sambucus nigra*), but here in the U.S. they are large shrubs (*Sambucus canadensis*). If you can grow one in the corner of your yard, they are easy and require little care. They don't like dryness, though—wherever you see them growing wild, there is groundwater less than six feet down, and they are known to grow right on the edge of swamps. So if you've got a mucky too-wet area, even one that floods a bit occasionally, filling it with elder bushes is a great answer.

Elder is a wonderful medicinal plant. She is so useful that she was called "the medicine chest of the common people". A syrup of her berries is just the thing for colds and flus—it is an immune booster, and expensive commercial versions are sold in pharmacies, but if you can find and pick elderberries, you can make your own.

In older times they called her Lady Ellhorn, and people asked her permission before they harvested her berries—or her flowers, or her bark, or all the other parts of her, each of which is useful for something different. In Europe, cutting elder trees for wood was discouraged, as the Elder spirit would curse you with illness. Long after other trees were no longer respected, people still asked the Elder for permission to touch any part of her. The spirit of Elder, who is a dignified old grandmother, was that intimidating. However, she was also known as the kindly Elder-Mother who healed children of fever and colds, as she is shown in Hans Christian Andersen's little-read short story "The Elder-Tree Mother".

In Germanic lore, the Elder-Mother is Holda's tree. (In Scandinavia, she was more associated with Hel, ruler of the Dead, and it was said that if you cut a hollow elder stem and looked through it, you would slide down into the Underworld.) Like the flax-spirit, sometimes Elder and Holda were quite conflated. So it makes sense that if you're making an Elderberry potion, you would call upon Holda to bless it.

You can also use dried elderberries for this potion, and they can even be ordered online, but I do love foraging for them. Two of my neighbors have Elder bushes, and they allow me to pick the bushes clean so long as I give them some of the syrup back. Usually I can make enough to keep multiple families mostly cold-free throughout a winter. Whichever you choose, you just put them in a pot of water about three times the volume of the berries, and simmer them over a low heat until the water has been reduced by half and the berries are mush. I add in a little cinnamon and nutmeg and cardamom and ginger and cloves, just to flavor the syrup a little more.

While I am standing over the syrup, I sing the following song five times. (I always feel like five is Holda's number.)

Grandmother Elder, keep me clear,
I will listen and I will hear.
Grandmother Holda, keep me sound,
Croon your blessings all around.
Grandmothers two, see us through.

Then you strain them out, very thoroughly. I put them in a cheesecloth and squeeze them until they are fairly dry and no moire liquid comes out. It stains the cheesecloth permanently, of course, so it is washed and put away to become the dedicated yearly elderberry draining cloth.

Next I put the liquid back on the stove and put in a good dollop of raw honey. This sweetens it—elderberries aren't terrible, but they aren't sweet like blueberries and strawberries, and some people object to the flavor. Raw honey also has other fine medicinal qualities that help people survive diseases. The ratio of honey to Elderberry juice should be around 1 cup of raw honey to a cup and a half of juice. Let it cool and see if it is the right syrupy consistency—it has to pour well, but not be too runny. Then bottle it and keep it in the refrigerator for the winter.

One of the families I provide this syrup to has a grandmother who is is diabetic and on a strict diet, and cannot have sucrose, even honey or maple syrup. She was unhappy but resigned that she couldn't have the syrup. (There is a sugar-free version of commercial Elderberry syrup on the market, but it is full of other chemicals.) A friend on the internet suggested that I check out some of the new somewhat-more-natural syrups that are made with monkfruit or stevia, which the lady could tolerate, and I made a batch with one of those syrups, the "vanilla" flavor. It came out wonderful, according to her, and so I give you this as a sugar-free alternative.

The prophylactic dosage is one spoonful every day, either at morning or night. It is entirely safe for children. If you feel a cold or some other illness coming on, increase the dosage to four spoonfuls spaced out over the day. I sing through the charm for Dame Elder and Holda every time I take it, and so do my children, because they think it's fun. May the two grandmothers keep you well!

Another Elderberry Charm for Holda

Raven Kaldera

I was taught that the wonderful syrup described by Mercy Karinczy was called Elderberry Rob, and I was taught to make it with sugar instead of honey, but I like the raw honey version better! Anyhow, Holda also gave me a charm to use when making and taking it, using some of the old folk names of Elder, and it goes like this:

Ellen, Ellen, Lady Ellhorn,
Eldest Moon and Magic Borne,
Holda, heal me, Ellhorn's mistress,
May the night give way to morn.

I also use it when making Green Elderleaf Ointment, which is a remedy for bruises, sprains, chilblains, and wounds. Ideally you're supposed to pick the young Elder leaves just before Beltane. The original recipe is 3 parts freshly gathered Elder leaves, 4 parts pork lard and 2 parts beef suet, both strained and white. Heat the leaves gently in the fat until the color is extracted, while saying the Elder charm below; then strain through a linen cloth and keep in the refrigerator.

You can use vegetable shortening if you want. I use coconut oil, which has the same sort of consistency at room temperature as animal fats, and keeps better for longer. I assume that in the old days, they used it up fairly quickly.

Our Yule Holda Rite

Raven Kaldera

Our Pagan church holds open high holidays, and we rotate ritual creators and cosmological pantheons—sometimes Greek, or Norse, or Celtic, or even Egyptian, depending on what the ritual-creation volunteer comes up with. For one Yule, we decided to focus entirely on the Germanic goddess Holda. The ritual would be held both inside and outside of a church member's house, and since anyone might come, it had to be simple and understandable.

We decided on a "wide game" format, where people move from station to station, and four members volunteered to be the "station keepers", each of them speaking about one aspect of Holda. I was one, and the others were women. We all wore white, or blue and white, with glittering silver-leaf wreaths on our heads. (I put mine on a wide-brimmed black hat.)

People arrived and parked, and were welcomed by a bonfire in the side yard where they warmed themselves. When it was time to start the ritual, a volunteer stood before the fire dressed in a long blue-and-white gown, her long silver hair flowing, and spoke of Holda as the goddess of Winter, who caused the snowfalls by beating her feather pillows. She had an old feather pillow that was falling apart, and everyone took a handful of feathers and threw them into the air, asking that the winter should please be kind to them.

Then they were led inside to the next station, in the living room. This was about Holda in her aspect as Spinner, and our volunteer was a member who knew how to handle a spinning wheel. As she spun, she explained all about Holda's aspect as a goddess of spinning and flax culture, and cut lengths of handspun thread off for each person. They were instructed to tie three knots in each end, and as they did it, to focus on the projects they had wanted to do last year, but which had fallen off their plates. They asked Holda for the energy and time and persistence to get those projects done, and then moved on to the kitchen.

The third volunteer was stirring pots of soup and spiced cider, and passed out soup and wassail to everyone. She explained Holda's aspect as hearthkeeper, and how she evolved into the German "kitchen witch". She also talked about the concept of the "kitchen witch" who does magic with household implements and substances, as opposed to the ceremonial magician who was usually no peasant-wife. She spoke of cooking food with intent, making healing brews, and the cauldron and spoon as cup and wand. Everyone was instructed to eat, drink, and focus on asking Holda to help them to nourish and heal others throughout the next year. Then they moved on to the dining area.

Here a volunteer spoke about Holda as the goddess of housecleaning and brooms, and how cleaning could be used mindfully as a focus for cleansing yourself (or a space) on a mental, emotional, and spiritual level. She passed out shiny pump-bottles labeled "Glass and Soul Cleaner", and instructed everyone to clean all the mirrors in their house while looking into them, and focusing on polishing up their own souls.

Then everyone went back outside to the fire, where I was waiting for them. I spoke of Holda as the goddess who took all the babies who died unbaptized, and that before Christianity put its own spoin on that, she would have been a maternal goddess who gathered in the souls of dead babes, which would probably have much comforted the grieving parents. I had made dozens of little "ghosts" out of white tissue paper with string loops to hang them, and I passed these out. I talked about how we all had lost dreams that we now knew would never happen, but we were reluctant to let go even though we knew we should, and that it was time to let go of at least one of those dead would-be manifestations. The folks were instructed to go hang their "dead baby" in the woods behind the house, where Holda would take them in and care for them. (We later gathered them after everyone left and put them into the wood cookstove, Holda's hearth.)

Then, after this serious ending, we sang songs around the fire while the food crew set out the potluck, and then went in to enjoy the feasting. Surprisingly, we heard from a number of people that they really became attached to the idea of Holda—and some were people you wouldn't expect to latch onto her, people who hadn't ever really dealt with Gods before. One told me at the next church event that they had been talking to Holda, and said, "Do you know what Holda says when you tell her that your life is a mess? She says, 'Why don't you clean your goddamn house?' So I did, and you know, it helped."

This has led, in our polytheistic multiple-cosmology pan-Pagan church, to many folks saying "Hail Holda!" whenever pre- or post-ritual cleaning needed to happen. She's become a watchword here, which makes me smile every time I hear it.

Glass and Soul Cleaner Recipe
Christine Banning

(*I was in charge of the Cleaning part of the Holda rite, and here's what I made to give out to the attendees.*)

Part 1: Standard home-made glass cleaner (approximate quantities per spray bottle since I'd made a huge batch).

1/2 tsp cornstarch
1 +1/3 TBSP rubbing alcohol
1 +1/3 TBSP vinegar
2/3 Cups water

Part 2: The Intention. The water was first warmed and infused with rosemary that I had planted and grown with intention/energy for home cleaning and for clarity of thought. I let it infuse for several hours, and had thanked Holda with much gratitude for Her help when adding it.

Holda's Sacred Places
Raven Kaldera

Every deity has places in the world that are sacred to them, whether or not we still remember them, or even knew them at all. There are a few places in the world which are connected with Holda's legends, and are sacred to Her. If you ever decide to make Holda pilgrimages, here are some goals to try for.

The Brocken

The highest peak of the Harz Mountains, and in northern Germany for that matter, the Brocken is Holda's Mountain. Supposedly it was used for seasonal Pagan rites during pre-Christian Saxon times, and portraits of Gods were said to be inscribed into the rock, although they were destroyed after the region converted. Throughout the medieval period and the following couple of centuries, it was said that witches gathered on the Brocken, to the point where it was general folk legend even in other countries. One outcrop is known as the Hexenaltar, or Witches' Altar; another is known as the Teufelskanzel, or Devil's Altar. Goethe popularized it as a witches' meeting place in his 1808 *Faust*.

The word *brocken* is an old German slang word for a big shapeless lump, which the Brocken certainly is. During the Victorian era, a hotel was built on the top and a narrow gauge railway put in. The railway is still going strong, but after World War II the Russians took over the East-German mountain and replaced with hotel with barbed wire and an armed lookout station. For decades the locals, who were used to climbing the mountain, could only look at it from a distance. In 1994 when the Berlin Wall fell and the soldiers moved on, four thousand people went out and climbed the Brocken in one day. Today every Walpurgisnacht—April 30—hundreds of people, often dressed in witch or monster or faery costumes, light bonfires on the Brocken and have a party. While it is strictly a secular celebration, it is good to know that the fires are happening once again. While any time (except the dead of winter when the train doesn't run) would be good for a Holda visit, Walpurgisnacht does honor her title as Queen of Witches.

Berchtesgaden

While many modern scholars claim that the name of this town comes from an old Romano-Germanic word *parach*, meaning "hay shed", the original etymology—now reduced to a "folk etymology"—claimed that it was named for Berchta, another name for Perchta. Regardless of which it is, this lovely Bavarian city can be honored in spirit as Perchta's *gaden* or "hut". Certainly the town has often had a Perchta folk procession with costumed "spirits" on Perchtertag (Shrovetide). The city has always been famous for its salt mines, which is a reminder of underground kobold spirits and somehow seems appropriate.

Hohensalzburg Castle

In the Austrian city of Salzburg, one of the biggest Perchtenlaufen or Perchten parades can be seen during

Carnival. There's a great white fortress/castle on the hill, built in the 11th century, and it is said that Perchta walks its halls at night, especially during the winter and at Shrovetide. While we have no evidence for or against this, the castle is a fascinating museum which includes medieval weapons.

Perchtenlaufen

Not a single place per se, the Perchtenlaufen or Perchten parades can be seen in various towns in the Alpine regions of Germany and Austria. Some parades are held in the winter, some in the spring; they are a mad array of folk costumes, with (of course) at least one giant, gnarled old woman in the middle.

Eschwege Landgrafschlossen

Landgrave Balthasar von Thuringia built a castle in Eschwege, in the German state of Hesse, in 1385. Parts of the original castle still remain, but much of it was renovated and rebuilt in the 15th, 18th, 19th, and 20th centuries. In the 1930s, a German architect named Sauter built a fanciful well in the courtyard which illustrates the story of Frau Holle; the "Frau Holle fountain" is mildly famous in the area.

Frau Holle Park, Lichtenau

This is a small park in Lichtenau, Germany, with a nice statue of Frau Holle shaking out her pillows, framed in an archway, and with a small sculptured well in front of her.

Hexenkopf Pillar

This is a natural rock formation in Williams' Township, Northampton County, Pennsylvania. The name translates to "Witches' Head", and was named by the Pennsylvania Deutsch, many of whom brought folk tales about Frau Holle over from Germany. It's said that the Hexenkopf Pillar is sacred to Holda, the Queen of Witches, and a century ago locals talked of seeing a white-clad woman wandering around it, especially on April 30th. A pool in the vicinity is used by modern practitioners for Holda holy water, and a cubic stone altar is used by them as an altar for rituals to Frau Holle.

Holda's Pillow

Heather Rohan Choppin named a mountain in the Beartooth Mountains in Montana "Holda's Pillow" in honor of the Winter Lady. They photographed it here:

Holda Mantra and Yantra

Raven Kaldera

(Recently we've been getting messages from polytheistic residents of India who would like to add the Northern Gods to their prayers. One asked for a mantra (chant) and a yantra (image to focus on), and so we are working on providing this in a format that would work for both cultural contexts for all the Northern Gods. Here is one for Holda, in Middle Germanic.)

Frouwa Holda, Sneolih Muotar, Spinnila Meistara, Holle, Holle,
Frouwa Holda, Sneolih Muotar, Spinnila Meistara, Holle, Holle, Heil.

Froo-wah Hol-dah, Shnay-oh-lee Moo-oh-tar,
Speen-eel-ah My-star-ah, Hoh-lay Hoh-lay,
Froo-wah Hol-dah, Shnayoh-lee Moo-oh-tar,
Speen-eel-ah My-star-ah, Hoh-lay Hoh-lay, Hyle.

Lady Holda, Snowy Mother, Spinning Mistress, Holle Holle,
Lady Holda, Snowy Mother, Spinning Mistress, Holle Holle, Hail.

The image to focus on while chanting is below:

Photo Attributions

All pictures below Creative Commons from Wikimedia Commons, and attributed as such.

- Opening page: Frau Holle statue by Viktor Donhauser: Willow
- Contents Page: Frau Holle Window Display: Aagnverglaser
- Pg. 10 Mother Huldra in Dutch fairy-tale park in Kaatsheuvel: Onderwijsgek
- Pg. 29 Scruffy Broom: Thomas Schmidt
- Pg. 39 Frau Holle Cottage: novaroos
- Pg. 48 "Four Feet High" by Heather Rohan Choppin, taken in Montana.
- Pg. 55 Frau Holle mural: Buchhändler
- Pg. 74 Wooden Frau Holle statue : Markus Goebel
- Pg. 77 Frau Holle Window Display 2: Aagnverglaser
- Pg. 81 Brooms: Vladimer Shioshvili
- Pg. 95 Brocken Mountain: Jörg Braukmann
- Pg. 96 Parade Perchta: Holger Uwe Schmitt
- Pg. 97 Frau Holle Fountain, Eschwege: Epsilon Eridani
- Pg. 97 Statue in Frau Holle Park: Kroll Markus
- Pg. 98 "Holda's Pillow" by Heather Rohan Choppin
- Pg. 100 Frau Holle mannekin: Johann Jaritz
- Pg. 101 Frau Holle Tree Statue: Angela Huster

All others public domain.

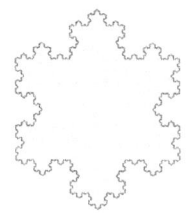

www.ingramcontent.com/pod-product-compliance
Lightning Source LLC
Chambersburg PA
CBHW020915090426
42736CB00008B/652